THE
UNIVERSE WITHIN

The Journey Through The Chakras

Paramahamsa Prajnanananda

The Universe Within

First Edition, March 2002
Second Edition, March 2003
Published by Prajna Publication, Diefenbachgasse 38/6, 1150 Vienna, Austria, Europe

Third Edition, May 2005
Published by Sai Towers Publishing
Copyright © 2005 Prajnana Mission

All rights reserved. This book may not be reproduced in whole or in part, or transmitted in any form, without written permission from the publisher, except by a reviewer who may quote brief passages in a review; nor may any part of this book be reproduced, stored in a retrieval system, or transmitted in any form or by any means electronic, mechanical, photocopying, recording, of other, without written permission from publisher.

Sai Towers Publishing
23/1142, VL Colony, Kadugudi, Bangalore 560 067 India
www.saitowers.com

A catalogue record of this book is available from the British Library.

Typeset in 11 point Book Antiqua

ISBN 81-7899-052-0

Printed and bound in India by Vishruti Prints

Dedication

On the auspicious 93rd birthday of My Beloved Gurudev Paramahamsa Hariharananda, from whom I learned the art of experiencing macrocosm in microcosm and the Divine everywhere; I offer this little flower at his divine feet and then pass it on to sincere seekers as a blessed flower for their spiritual evolution.

humble

Prajnanananda

Acknowledgement

No good work is accomplished without cooperative effort and the blessings of God and Gurus. My sincere love and appreciation to one and all who have helped me in various ways to bring out this book.

God will bless them,
Prajnanananda

Foreword

Paramahamsa Prajnananandaji's latest release is a fascinating look at the similarities between the outer universe and the inner workings of the human body. This is definitely not the usual metaphysical book. Rather than concentrating on *yogic* postures and scientific expositions on the *chakras*, Prajnananandaji focuses on the essential question: How can we achieve immediate and lasting happiness?

He describes how the five elements of space, air, fire, water and earth constitute the entire physical universe, and how those same elements constitute the human body. *The Universe Within* takes us on a fascinating tour of the inner universe of the body, the mind, the *chakras* and our own intricate personality traits, which we have the power to transform.

Among the most interesting and unique sections of the book are the description of the various elements and their attributes, as well as the striking parallels between physical features of the Earth and the inner workings of the human body. Prajnananandaji presents the ancient wisdom of the seers in everyday language, using unusual allegories and eloquent metaphors. He emphasizes the need for all of us to become spiritual scientists, who are able to connect inner and outer phenomenon in order to achieve lasting happiness, evolution and growth. Whether you are a rocket scientist, a star athlete, an executive, an accomplished housewife or a skilled factoryworker, this is a book that will help you tap the immense potential contained within you.

The Editor

CONTENTS

1. **Creation: Earth, Water, Fire, Air, Space**   1
   Energy and Consciousness - God's Creation - The Elements and Their Attributes - Combination of Elements - The Inner Himalayas - The Three Holy Rivers - Scientific Spirituality - The Lotus, the Conch, the Mace and the *Chakra*

2. **The Monkey Mind in the Body Forest**   13
   Three Bodies - The City of Many Doors - The Gross Body - The Subtle Body - The Causal Body - Three States of Existence - Five Sheaths - The Three Qualities - The Monkey Mind - The Monk and the Maiden - Inner Battle: The Struggle for Perfection

3. **The Seven Chakras**   25
   Practical Benefits - *Muladhara Chakra* - Acquiring Wealth - Gold or Dust? - Ganesha - Receiving Knowledge - Energizing the Body - Observing the Mind - *Swadhisthana Chakra* - Sex and Food - Buddha's Realization - Not Enough Salt - The Seduction of Taste - Knowing What We Want - Yayati's Curse - *Manipura Chakra* - Food and Temptation - We Eat Food and Food Eats Us - The deluded Saint - The Fire of Illumination and Elimination - The Creative Knot - The Inner Pilgrimage - *Anahata Chakra* - Sons of Vayu - Emotional Disorders - Universal Love - Vishnu, The Symbol of Tolerance - Centre of Transformation - *Vishuddha Chakra* - Religious Intolerance - A Dip in Ganga - Nilakantha: Blue Throat - *Ajna Chakra* - The Inner Anvil - The Third Eye - Pole Star - Knot of Liberation - *Sahasrara Chakra* - The Vast Inner Sky - Polarity - Beyond Name and Form - *Chakra* Purification - Stars and Planets

4. **The Perfect Family**   79
   Patience as the Father - Forgiveness as the Mother - Peace as the Spouse - Truth as the Child - Compassion as the Sister - Controlled Mind as the Brother - The Story of Suka - The Earth as a Bed - Space as the Garment - Wisdom as Food - Family of Shiva

5. **Meditation: Practice and Benefits**   88
Where to Meditate: Forest, House or Mind? - The Proper Posture - The Proper Seat - Meditation as Worship - How to Meditate - The Need for a Teacher - The Basic Method - Having a Road Map - Daily Practice - The Weed-Covered Pond - Keeping the Channel Open - The Physical Benefits - Joy beyond description - The Ocean and the Waves - The Four Stages of Spiritual Evolution - Churn the Ocean of Life

6. **Tapping the Source**   103
The Human Miracle - Hidden Treasures - Dive Deep, Fly High - The Dazzling Jewel - Stop the Play of Mind - Blissful State

CHAPTER 1

CREATION
EARTH, WATER, FIRE, AIR, SPACE

From that Brahman indeed, which was this Self, ether arose, from air came fire, from fire came water and from water came the earth.

(Taitariya Upanisad, II-I:3)

When we look at the world around us, we are stunned by the sheer multiplicity of creation. The stars, the planets, the oceans, the forests, the thousands of species of flora and fauna, the vastness of space and the incredible beauty of our own planet Earth with its soaring peaks, its lush valleys, its magnificent oceans and its fertile plains, all these are breathtaking wonders. We are usually too busy with our lives, with our daily routine-business of working, having fun, eating and sleeping, to look around and take notice of God's handiwork. We only seem to notice nature's powerful beauty on those rare occasions when we are particularly struck by the beauty of a sunset or overwhelmed by the view of a sapphire expanse of water, when we look at a glittering rainbow peeping through black clouds or when, on a summer day, we sit on a soft green lawn and we happen to feel the warmth of the sun caressing our skin. Perhaps we react even more when we are frightened out of our complacency by the sudden shock of an earthquake and thousands die, or by the news of a hurricane which has left millions of people floundering in disaster and made billions of dollars of damage. Finally we are forced to come face to face with the power and the presence of the elements.

Nature's beauty always surrounds us, it always is around us and within us, but we walk through it blindly, lost in the maze of our convoluted thoughts, desires, hopes and fears. God gave us the Earth where to live, filling it in abundance with trees, flowers, fruits, animals, mountains, rivers, snow, rain, wind and fire...but what did we do?

We shunned the freedom man had been gifted with, we ran away from it almost in fear and started building small or huge cages made of steel and concrete and many-storied skyscrapers; we built cages which stand still and even metal cramped cages which move us from place to place, which keep us firmly imprisoned until we die. We have shun the wide open spaces and, having retreated from that lack of restrictions, we hide away in our burrows, like frightened rabbits, emerging only to eke out our livelihood in similar burrows or to shop for necessities. We have built huge malls, where to spend our free time wandering among those high-tech tunnels, we ourselves have built and are so proud of. How can the glitter and glamour of the man-made world compare to the majesty of God's creation?

The Earth watches patiently while we destroy her inch by inch, burning down forests, polluting the air, creating deadly weapons and poisoning her waters. God watches sadly, waiting for us to stop and open our eyes, still the frenzied thoughts which drive us to run madly about and listen...listen to the music which is more beautiful than any symphony, look at the beauty which is more riveting than any work of art and breathe deeply the celestial air which is scented by love. Love is always there, even in cities, even in crowds, but we drown it with our own noise and all our activity and commotion. We act and we react, we want and we despise, we desire and we hate, due to our selfish, narrow and blind approach towards this very precious life we were given, forgetting that to love and being loved by God is the most marvelous gift.

Our minds are full of desires. What are desires? Desires are nothing more than an itch that needs to be scratched and, although there is relief in removing what momentarily troubles us, surely that cannot be real happiness. What is happiness? What most people normally call happiness is merely the cessation of misery, but real supreme happiness is far more than this. God wanted to give us much more, therefore He gave us all we needed in order to achieve the state of supreme happiness. Not only did God gift human beings with the stunning phenomena of the outer universe, but He also gave man the magnificence of that very phenomenal universe reflected within man himself.

Energy and Consciousness

Whether we acknowledge them or not, the elements are always present, surging, clashing, mingling, and subsiding around us. It is from the five fundamental elements that creation began and continues to occur. The entire cosmos consists of the play of energy and consciousness. Energy is manifested in many ways, forms, and names. If God is considered the formless aspect, then the elements are considered the embodiments of God's formless energy. In Hindu mythology, the form and the formless are represented by Shiva and Shakti, consciousness and energy. While Shiva is the formless absolute, the unchanging consciousness behind creation, Shakti, his mate, is the boundless energy of creation itself, the constantly shifting and metamorphous nature of the five elements. The beauty and power of creation are represented through the dance of Shiva and Shakti, consciousness and energy.

God's Creation

The Lord God formed man from the dust of the ground and breathed into his nostrils the breath of life and man became a living being. (Torah 2/7)

Creation is the play of cosmic energy being manifested in the form of matter and memory, both combined together with consciousness. Each human body, otherwise called the temple of the Divine, is made of dust and merges back into dust after death. Dust symbolizes the five elements of earth, water, fire, air and sky.

In God's creation birds are to fly in the sky, fish are to swim and dive in water, reptiles and rodents are to live in holes in the earth and wild animals are to roam freely in the dense forests. It is only human beings whom God created in His own image and gave them the supreme skill, which no other animal possesses, the power to think and create. Man can fly like birds, swim like fish and he can even go underground into the deep mines he himself has dug. Man has utilized all these skills, but unfortunately, he has not tried hard enough to reach the real source and experience the state of inner fulfillment.

Inner fulfillment may be achieved exploring the hidden treasure of breath. Breath is the mystifying and marvelous blessing of God, which enables us to manifest our love through the experience of calmness and peace. How beautiful it is to be born a human being who can help himself and others make the inner and outer universe more spellbinding and exquisite.

The Elements and Their Attributes

The *Vedas*, the ancient Hindu scriptures, which are considered as the timeless wisdom that was revealed to the calm and tranquil mind of the seers, explain that first there was the Absolute. From the Absolute Truth, came space, for without space nothing can be created. Space is defined as that which has the attribute of sound and which provides space for all things that have a form. From space came air. Air has two attributes, it possesses the quality of touch, as well as the quality of sound carried over from the space in which it was born. From air came fire, which has three attributes, sight as well as the touch of air and the sound of space. Fire produced water, which carries taste as well as the other three attributes of sight, touch and sound. From water came the earth, which consists of all the five attributes: smell, taste, sight, touch and sound.

The Combination of Elements

The five elements are said to have been the first created in their subtle form and, by combining among themselves, they have become the gross elements we are able to perceive. In Sanskrit the process by which the subtle elements combine to become the perceptible gross elements is called *panchikarana*. This process takes place by a five-fold division and combination. The unit of each subtle element divides into two.

One half remains intact while the other half divides itself into four parts which contain one eighth of the original unit. In the next step each half combines with an eighth of all the other four elements to form a unit of the gross element. Thus, each element is a combination of half of itself with one eighth of each of the other four.

Example: a unit of air consists of half air and one eighth of each of the other four elements; ether, fire, water and earth. Just as the Sun and its energy are one, God and these elements are also one. The *Vedas* connect these five elements to man and state that – from the earth with its five attributes comes food, food is then transformed into seed, including human seed, the semen and the ovum, which in turn gives rise to the conception of a human being. Thus man too is composed of the self-same five elements which make up the external universe. These five elements also constitute the universe within. The *Vedas* declare that whatever is seen in the cosmos can also be seen in the human body and the *Jnana Sankalini Tantra* teaches us that the entire universe resides within the human body.

This may seem incredible at first. How can the vast magnitude of the entire universe possibly be contained within the relatively tiny human body? The Vedic seers have a precise and scientific explanation.

The Inner Himalayas

Like the earth, also the body has a north and a south pole and the entire cosmos is represented in between these two poles. Just as with our eyes open we can gaze at the external sky, with our eyes closed we can view and admire the inner sky. Sometimes,

CREATION

in the deep concentration of silent meditation, dazzling lights and stars are visible in that inner vastness. Just as there is air outside, air is circulated throughout the whole body via the breath and just as on planet earth water flows through the rivers, in our body, blood flows through the veins and arteries.

In the outer world, on this planet, the Himalayas are the tallest as well as the youngest existing mountains. Ever since India crashed into the rest of Asia, thus forming the Himalayas, these mountains have continued to rise imperceptibly year after year. How does this relate to the body? In Sanskrit, the spine is called the *Merudanda*. *Meru* means mountain and *danda* may be translated as the vertical axis. In the human body, there are seven mountains. Out of these seven mountains, the oldest is the heart and the tallest and the youngest is the brain.

Our brain, just like the Himalayas, is constantly growing, but it is not only growing as physical matter, it grows in memory as memory ceaselessly goes on expanding. We may, therefore, assert that our brain has the Himalayan potential for growth, expansion and experience.

There is a further similarity between the Himalayas and the human brain. The word Himalayas can be broken up into two words, *Hima* meaning cold or snow, and *alaya,* meaning house. The Himalayas are a cold region and also the human brain is a cool place. When the mind goes upward toward the brain and intellect, it becomes cool and tranquil, and when it travels downward toward the pull of the senses, it becomes hot and agitated. Even in the external world, the higher one ascends, the cooler the temperature becomes. In the same way, the mind needs to be elevated in order to keep cool.

The Three Holy Rivers

Just as from earthly mountains many rivers flow, in our body we have many nerve channels which may be compared to rivers. Continuing the analogy of the Himalayas, the human brain can be compared to the snowy peaks, the source of water. From the brain originate twelve pairs of cranial nerves along with groups of sensory and motor nerves which contain a flow of information which travels to and fro. This information creates transformation. When we receive some good news our faces are transformed with joy and, when we receive bad news, our faces turn gloomy. Our breathing, our pulse, and our emotions are all affected by the information we receive or the information we send through these channels.

In the body, there are seven mountains or *chakra*s situated along the spine, and through these mountains, the nerve currents flow like rivers. Among these rivers, three are as vital to the body as the physical rivers of the Ganga, the Yamuna, and the Saraswati are to India. In the *Vedas*, these three vital rivers or nerve channels are called *Ida, Pingala,* and *Sushumna. Ida* starts from the left side of the brain and extends along the left side of the spine. *Pingala* is on the right and in between is the invisible channel of *Sushumna.* The sages of long ago found that in India, there were two visible holy rivers, the Ganges and the Yamuna, while beneath them there flowed an invisible undercurrent which they dubbed the Saraswati.

The channels in the body correspond to these three holy rivers. The river Ganges is reflected within our body as the *Ida* channel, the Yamuna as *Pingala,* and the Saraswati river, which flows unseen underneath, as *Sushumna.* It is only recently that

CREATION

geologists have discovered that there is indeed a water current that flows below the river Ganges, which is so powerful and rich that, if it were explored, it would have the potential to solve the water crisis in India. In the same way, while the left side of the body is *Ida* and the right side is *Pingala,* it is the underlying *Sushumna* which is most powerful. Just as the Saraswati river lies untapped in India, most human beings have yet to tap the incredible reservoir of energy which lies in the *Sushumna* within them. Most people function on the surface, using the visible energy sources. Those who do explore the uncharted regions of the *Sushumna* obtain tremendous energy and peace.

Scientific Spirituality

Modern scientists attempt to harness the outer elements, in order to make our life in the world easier and comfortable and provide means to facilitate our daily struggle. The seers or *Yogis* of ancient India worked with the five elements within the body and discovered ways to make our inner life happier. It is essential to discover the role of the elements and keep them in a balanced, harmonious and peaceful state both on the outside and in the inside. Science and spirituality should be harmonized; science without spirituality can loose direction and create a great chaos, but on the other hand, if the focus is on spiritual development alone, there would not be much benefit for the society. It would be essential for the harmonious evolution of today's world to have scientists who, like the sages of long ago, are able to combine their knowledge of the outer universe with the insights of their inner universe and use this information to facilitate both inner and outer progress.

The Lotus, the Conch, the Mace and the Chakra

In Indian mythology among the three great deities or trinity there is a god called Vishnu who has four hands. In each of his four hands, he holds a different object: a *chakra* or disk, a conch, a lotus and a mace. Similarly, to protect and maintain our life energy, we need four things and each one is symbolized by the objects Vishnu holds in his four hands.

The first is the lotus. The lotus is one of nature's most beautiful flowers. Lotuses bloom most profusely in muddy lakes and ponds. While their roots remain in the sticky mud and the stem is submerged in the water, the flower itself remains above the water, aloof from its muddy surroundings. Our lives can be compared to the life of a lotus which, though dependent on the mud and the water for sustenance, only looks at the Sun. The muddy riverbed can be likened to the material sustenance we need to survive in the world, the water of love, which is so essential for our growth and the emotional aspect of our lives.

If we are to truly flourish, neither material satisfaction, nor emotional support are enough, so we should be like the lotus and focus only on the spiritual sun in order to maintain our purity and beauty.

The mace is the second symbol in Vishnu's hands. The mace is a weapon that ancient warriors used for killing and crushing their enemies. In the spiritual struggle, the mace represents the need to crush our ego and eliminate all our negative qualities.

The conch is the third symbol in Vishnu's hand. The conch is a very difficult instrument to blow and therefore it symbolizes

CREATION

thorough control over one's breath. Breath control, as I will explain later on, is the essential means to attain inner peace. The second meaning of the conch is the quality of the sound it produces, it is called the *nadabrahma*, the divine sound one hears deep within during meditation.

The last object in Vishnu's hands is the *chakra* or disc. The *chakra* symbolizes more than one spiritual aspect. In Vishnu's hand, the *chakra* constantly spins and it thus represents the endless wheel of time or the wheel of life. In Buddhist literature, the *chakra* is denominated *dharmachakra,* the wheel of morality. The English term for *chakra* is the wheel. The wheel symbolizes movement, progress and evolution. According to the *Upanishads*, the body is the chariot, the senses are the horses, the intellect serves as the reins and the soul is the charioteer. The body chariot with its seven wheels or *chakra*s is a special vehicle, which helps us to grow and evolve.

Let us take the example of a car. Unless all its wheels are in good conditions and often duly checked, one may risk an accident while driving at high speed on a highway, but if one keeps them regularly under control, the car will safely reach its destination. Similarly, the wheels or *chakra*s in the body car always need to be in good shape and under control in order to help us achieve our goals.

The term *chakra* can also be translated as disc, a weapon used in ancient times to slice through the enemy in battle. A *yogi*, through meditation and a conscientious lifestyle, can cut through all the obstacles in his life and reach the state of inner awakening.

A *chakra* can also be the potter's wheel, where many clay objects are formed under different names, and all become useful to contribute to the advancement of human civilization.

In this book, I will be focusing on the importance of the charkas within our own bodies. *Chakras* are the potential energy centres with a storehouse of strength, stability, knowledge and love each person needs. When these centres are seldom used, they rust and become useless. Each human scientist, sitting in his body chariot, should know the art of directing his life energy towards his evolution and growth. Each human life is full of the power of creation through the *chakras* in the spine and the brain. Purposeful living, careful undertaking and practical effort bring forth success. Each *chakra* represents certain human qualities and can be the source of endless misery if left uncontrolled. On the other hand, by following the simple principles outlined in the following chapters, not only are we able to understand the motivating force which drives us to do whatever we do, but we can also learn to direct and control that force in order to achieve immeasurable and endless bliss.

The sooner we understand that we ourselves contain the entire cosmos; that we have the source of all happiness within us, that we already possess all the objects we could desire, the sooner we can obtain the peace we seek. Rather than running endlessly after what dazzles us in the exterior world, we need to learn how to fix our attention on the magnificent universe within.

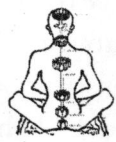

CHAPTER 2

THE MONKEY MIND IN THE BODY FOREST

By mind alone, is this to be achieved. There is no multiplicity here. Whoever perceives anything like multiplicity here, goes from death to death.

(*Katha Upanishad,* II-I-11)

A forest in the wilderness is full of beauty. There are high mountains, gurgling rivers filled with life-giving waters, fresh green grass and sheltering trees. At the same time, the forest is full of dangers as ferocious beasts are roaming free and hunting for prey. In the same way, the body forest contains both good and bad elements, our positive qualities as well as our negative ones.

In the *Genesis*, God asked man to rule over the wilds of the earth, the birds in the air and the fish living in the water. Basically, the tool we were given to rule over this 'body forest' is our mind. The mind, however, tends to be like a monkey and needs to be trained carefully.

The body is a beautiful instrument, it may be compared to the bamboo flute Krishna used to carry everywhere with Him. If we observe Krishna's bamboo flute, there are seven holes and He plays closing and opening six of the holes with His fingers, but the seventh hole always remains close to His lips. Similarly, God has gifted us with a spine that may be compared to a flute; this spine, instead of holes, has six *chakras*, the centres of money, sexual activity, food, emotion, religion and spirituality. All these six *chakras* are necessary, but they should be skillfully played upon and should be closed and opened in moderation. As Krishna keeps the seventh hole to His lips, God blows His breath into the human body through the seventh hole. Each human life is a *Bhagavad Gita*, read it, sing it, enjoy it and make it handsome. Each tune is different and hauntingly attractive, but only when all seven centres of this human flute are in harmony, does the divine song of God emerge and this song leads us to absolute bliss. All other tunes, in comparison, become merely entertaining little melodies and, though they may have appeared attractive, melodious and captivating, they cannot stand the test of time and soon reveal themselves to be unfinished and incomplete.

This is how the senses and the mind play in each human being. Sankara, in his authoritative and fascinating *Vivekachoodamani*, gives us examples directly from nature describing how certain species meet their death due to extreme attachment to one or the other of the five senses. The deer is fascinated by the melodious sound of the horn and, when the hunter blows it to attract him in the open, not being aware of the danger that lurks behind such a melodious sound, runs towards the music and becomes the target of the hunter. Many insects are attracted and trapped by the brightness of light, so their own sense of sight becomes their downfall. Elephants are fascinated and mesmerized by touch, bees by their acute sense of smell and fish by a tasty bait. In the same way we become entranced and captured by trivial worldly musical fragments, illusive lights, feelings, perfumes and tastes.

Most of us are extremely attached to our bodies. The body's pleasure or pain, its comfort or discomfort, its hunger, thirst or sexual fulfillment are the driving factors in our lives. Our work, our pastimes, emotions and thoughts are mostly spent on catering to the needs of our body but, although we focus so intensely on the body's physical needs, most of us are unaware of the body's actual intrinsic potential and how to use it.

Three Bodies

Very few people know that rather than one body, we actually have three: the gross body, to which we are so inordinately and exceedingly attached, the astral body, which can be defined as a person's mental makeup or personality and the causal body, which is comprised of our ignorance and knowledge.

The gross body constantly undergoes change and, whether we are willing to face it or not, it is perishable. Changes relentlessly occur everyday; old cells die and new cells form ad infinitum. What does not change is the formless aspect, that which constitutes the self, the soul.

When you ask a person what his name is, irrespective of what stage of life he may be in, either a child, an adult or an elderly person, the answer will always be the same: "I am so and so".

The body undergoes many changes; the child becomes a youth and the youth soon becomes mature and then an old person, but only the sense of 'I' remains always the same, so it is imperative to realize that there exists an unchanging and a changing aspect in our lives. Unfortunately people mistakenly cling to the changing aspect and, eventually, feel cynically disillusioned by life because they have been paying attention only to its illusory wrong aspect, the changeless nature that lies behind all changes.

The City of Many Doors

In the Vedas, the human body is described as a city of many doors. We only live in this city with many doors for a short period of time as in the body, which is the temple of God, the soul resides only temporarily and, as the span of life is so short, therefore we need to gain the maximum benefit from these few years God has allotted us.

There are nine doors in the body. These doors are the two eyes, two nostrils, two ears and the mouth. Seven out of the nine doors are present in the face, the other two doors are the genital organs and the anus.

We have five organs of perception and five organs of action. The five organs of perception are: the eyes to see, the ears to hear, the nose to smell, the tongue to taste and the skin to feel and touch. The five of action are: a mouth to speak, hands to work, feet to walk, the genital organs to procreate and the anus to excrete waste matter.

The elements in the body vibrate in two different ways and have two specific functions. Space is active in the ears in order to hear and in the throat to produce sound. Air is active in the skin to enable us to feel when we touch and in the hands to increase our sensitivity for our work skills. Fire is active in the eyes to allow us to see and in the feet to walk. Water is active in the mouth to enhance the taste buds and in the genitals. Earth is active in the nose to empower us to smell and in the anus. When the organs of perception and action come in contact with external objects, we perceive the opposites of heat and cold, unhappiness and happiness, pleasure and pain. Since the human body is prone to disease and deterioration, it is imperative that we take good care of the gross body. Although most people are aware of the need to eat healthy food and exercise to keep in shape the gross body, they usually totally ignore the other two bodies, the subtle and the causal bodies.

The Gross Body

The gross body of each human being is composed of the five elements, and, as everybody has these five same elements in common, the question arises as to why we are all so different. The answer lies in the proportion of these same elements present in the gross body as well as in the makeup of our subtle or astral body. The astral body of each person contains the various tendencies, formed from previous lives' repeated experiences, thoughts and deeds. Hence the distinction in constitutions and human beings' variety of dispositions and temperaments. The gross body is the physical body, which can be easily perceived by the five sense organs of sight, smell, touch, taste and hearing. The gross body undergoes six modifications: birth, existence, growth, maturity, decay and death. The gross body is also the instrument and the medium for the fulfillment of many ambitions.

The Subtle Body

The subtle body, also known as the astral body, can be explained and described as the combination of senses, vital breath and experiences man receives through the mind and intellect and which constitute our own unique personality. The subtle body is much larger than the gross body since it encompasses the mind. While the gross body is limited in its activities, with our mind or subtle body it is possible to travel anywhere at lightning speed, yet most of us do not know how to utilize the astral body to its full capacity. The astral body is at its most efficient and healthiest point when the mind is pure, clean and concentrated. The immense spiritual energy, which lies hidden and untapped in the subtle body, if properly used, will enable us to experience inexplicable joy and bliss.

The Causal Body

Finally, the causal body can be defined as the body of ignorance as well as knowledge that we carry with us. It is that state in which we have neither knowledge of the physical body nor of the underlying self. It is the state of complete self-absorption and ignorance. This very ignorance covers our other two bodies and is the primary cause for our continuous cycle of birth, death and suffering. Once ignorance is eliminated, we are free and liberated. Ordinary worldly knowledge, no matter how extensive, cannot remove this body of ignorance. It is only self-knowledge born of deep analysis and perception, which may lead to true liberation. The *Vedas* assert that man can realize the Absolute Truth only when he has transcend all the three bodies.

Three States of Existence

To summarize the activities of the three bodies, we have three states of existence. Every day, we experience the wakeful, dream and deep sleep states. In each of these states, we use one or more of the three bodies that we possess. In the wakeful state, the body, mind and senses are active. In the dream state, the gross body is dormant, but the astral body as well as the causal body are active. In the deep sleep state, we are in a blissful state of unawareness, in which we know neither pain nor pleasure. It is the play of the causal body, being free from the gross as well as the astral body.

The Five Sheaths

Since the human body is composed of the five elements, it is also sustained and regulated by the very same five elements byproducts: food, drink, temperature, breath and movement. Not only is each body triplicate in nature as it is manifested in the gross, astral and causal bodies, but it is also encompassed by five sheaths that are called *pancha kosas*. These are the *annamaya kosa* (food sheath), the *pranamaya kosa* (vital air sheath), the *manomaya kosa* (mental sheath), the *vijnanamaya kosa* (intellectual sheath), and the *anandamaya kosa* (blissful sheath).

The food sheath is more gross and physical in nature, while the other sheaths are more subtle and astral. When, along with these five sheaths, there is a play of consciousness, life becomes more vibrant and attractive.

The sheaths correspond to the different particular states and activities of the body. The physical sheath is associated with the physical body and the wakeful state, and all the inherent sense activities. The vital air sheath is associated with breathing; the mental and the intellectual sheaths control one's emotional and intellectual propensities. The blissful state is that ineffable state of happiness and inner calmness one experiences in deep sleep or in a state of deep meditation.

When these five sheaths have been thoroughly purified by concentration and meditation, the light of the soul manifests more clearly in our life through all of our own body's activities. As a result, life becomes more divine and peaceful.

When these five sheaths are cleansed through concentration and meditation, the light of the soul is manifested more clearly in the life and activities of our body. As a result, life becomes more divine and peaceful.

The Three Qualities

Human nature and behaviour are the outcome of the three qualities or *gunas*, present within each of us. People may be divided into groups depending on their mind's predominant quality. The three *gunas* or qualities are *sattva*-purity, *rajas*-activity and *tamas*-inertia. Each of us has these three qualities in varying proportions. When a person is *sattvic* or pure, one tends to be more contemplative, mature and gives priority to the real values and goals of life. When a person is mostly *rajasic*, one is very active and ambitious. When a person is mostly *tamasic*, one is often lazy and dull, has little or no ambition at all and usually compromises life's intrinsic true values.

The Monkey Mind

The human body is the playground of the mind. The mind can go in either direction, up or down. The mind experiences the world with the help of the five elements, the ten senses and breath. We spend most of our lives busily drowning out the silent splendour that lies within a thousand conflicting desires, agonies and doubts that stem from the monkey mind, which is always restless and impatient. Perhaps, while we were still in our mother's womb, we still experienced and were aware of the divine magnificence and bathed in its glorious light, but the very moment we were born, the mind took over, frantic, full of urges, a slave to the senses, craving pleasure and comfort from outer sources.

Just as a baby reaches with longing to his mother for milk, warmth and love, as soon as we are born, we begin the never-ending journey towards an ever-elusive happiness. The love and comfort we crave, draw us along a path of pain and pleasure, happiness and unhappiness, torment and fulfillment, which for every scant drop of fleeting satisfaction, drown us in an ocean of misery and longing because the mind, never being contented, endlessly multiplies our misery.

The Monk and the Maiden

There is a story from the *Puranas* that illustrates the nature of the mind. Two young monks who had been taught neither to look nor touch a woman, were sitting on the banks of Ganga, when a young lady fell in the river and showed serious signs she was on the point of drowning. Of the two monks only one jumped into the water to rescue the drowning young lady without hesitating one single moment as he considered it his fundamental duty to save her life. He rescued her and brought her to the shore and revived her using the mouth-to-mouth resuscitation technique. The other monk remained motionless and was shocked by his friend's action as he considered it to be against the principles of monkhood. The lady left after having thanked them profusely and the two monks returned to their ashram. On the way back the second monk scolded the first stressing that he had gone against all the monastic rules and their Guru's recommendations. He said: "You touched a woman's body, you embraced her, you kissed her!!" On hearing all this the first monk laughed and answered: "After having rescued her, I left that young lady on the banks of the river, while you, my friend, are bringing her with you back to the ashram!"

The mind is infinitely more powerful than the physical body. It attaches itself to various objects and to a multiplicity of memories, it moves from place to place at lightning speed, and is full of thoughts and cravings that constantly demand to be fulfilled. The mind plays with our doubts and feelings deep within just as it plays with the cravings and desires we project towards the external world.

Inner Battle—The Struggle for Perfection

Another name for the human spine in Sanskrit is *Merudanda*, which means staff. Even many Bible stories describe Moses and Jesus holding a staff in their hand and many Indian monks still carry a staff or a stick in their hands as the staff is a symbol representing the spine: by holding the staff, they are controlling the spine. It is said that one who holds this *Merudanda* and consciously regulates each of the seven *chakra*s, can attain absolute control over his mind.

The human race has always been engaged in continuous battles in order to acquire more and more material wealth, but the real battle is not in the outside world, but it is a constant inner struggle:

Put on the full Armour of God so that you can take your stand against the devil's schemes. For the struggle is not against flesh and blood"

(*The Holy Bible*, Ephessians 10-18).

Many of the Hindu scriptures describe the innumerable battles that constantly take place within. Among all the mythological battles, the ones described in the *Ramayana* and in the *Mahabharata* are the most prominent and inspiring as they are symbolic of the human evolution and the absolute need to subjugate one's lower propensities.

Both these famous battles illustrate the need to kill the demonic nature within in order to awaken one's spiritual energy. In the *Ramayana*, Rama wants to get his wife, Sita, back by conquering Ravana. Sita represents peace and Ravana is portrayed with ten heads to represent man's ten sense organs. Ravana, the demon who had kidnapped Sita (peace), is not part of an outside tangible world, but lies within each of our ten sense organs. Each one of his 10 heads is as equally powerful as each sense organ that kidnaps our inner peace by making our mind run after sense objects.

In the battle of the *Mahabharata*, the hundred *Kauravas* represent our inner negative qualities of passion, restlessness, anger, ego, jealousy and the incessant flow of thoughts that run in ten different directions corresponding to the ten sense organs. The *Pandavas*, on the contrary, are less in number and represent the rare good qualities we possess.

This constant battle between our positive and negative qualities relentlessly and persistently goes on in each one of us. In the battle, sometimes some good qualities are suppressed and negative qualities rule and sometimes the positive ones win the conflict.

When life is full of love there is no anger and no ego, when the mind is fully engaged with positive thoughts, there is no door open to allow negative, idle thoughts. An idle mind is indeed a devil's workshop as whatever we do appears first in the form of a thought. A thought is like the seed we plant, the sprout is the result of our work and the tree or the fruit is the final manifestation, so every human mind can be a divine kingdom in heaven or a devilish place in hell and the choice is totally ours. If one is after spiritual growth, one should be very careful about one's thoughts as these can make one's life either delightfully divine or full of negativity.

Within each one of us there is unbounded Divinity. To experience our own Divinity, there is no other way than meditation. If we do not purify our minds, we will not progress and this overwhelming and constant process is the unique and steady battle to attain the ultimate perfection.

CHAPTER 3

THE SEVEN CHAKRAS

> The One is revealed within the effulgent golden light. The Absolute Brahman, who is Self-luminous, pure consciousness, who is the light of lights and whose supreme reality is known to men of Self-realization.
>
> *(Mundaka Upanishad, II-II-9)*

A myriad books have been written on the mysteries of the *chakras* and how they can be used for healing oneself. This is not one of those books, it rather focuses on detailed insights which clarify how working on each one of these centers of energy, may influence the seekers' spiritual awakening. Some books depict the *chakras* as lotuses with a varying number of petals withholding strange powers, other books decry them as mystical nonsense and completely lacking any actual physical basis. Other sources warn of the dangers involved in arousing the *kundalini* energy which is said to be stored in serpent form at the base of the spine.

Rather than dwell on the metaphysical subtleties of the *chakras,* or on intricate descriptions of their forms, on the number of petals in each lotus or on other such useless information, this book focuses on the various human qualities associated with each energy centre and points out how to recognize, control and direct the peculiarities of each *chakra* so that the seeker may travel safely towards the goal of absolute happiness.

Practical Benefits

The main aim of this book is to stress the practical benefits one may derive from developing one's *chakra*s through spiritual endeavors and explain how one may gain wealth, fame, emotional fulfillment, creative inspiration and finally spiritual realization by understanding and energizing the *chakra*s.

Each *chakra* is a storehouse of immense potential, which can fulfill our deepest desires or plunge us into the deepest despair. Once we learn the art of controlling these *chakra*s through the process of meditation, there is no limit to the infinite possibilities for physical, material, emotional, and spiritual success.

Although it is true that these *chakra*s or energy centres cannot be anatomically pinpointed, it is also true that there are seven main *chakra*s along the human spine formed by the myriad of nerve channels flowing down from the brain when they get very close to each other at certain points along the spine. When this happens, new circuits or magnetic fields are created. These magnetic fields or *chakra*s are subtle energy centres in the spine.

There are seven major energy centres, which are called either *chakra*s or lotuses and, in modern times, have also been referred to as plexuses. They are:

- *Muladhara chakra*, coccygial or money centre in the coccyx (base of the spine).
- *Swadhisthana chakra*, sacral or second centre in the sacral region.
- *Manipura chakra*, lumbar or naval centre in the lumbar region.
- *Anahata chakra*, dorsal or heart centre in the dorsal region.
- *Vishuddha chakra*, neck or cervical centre in the cervix.

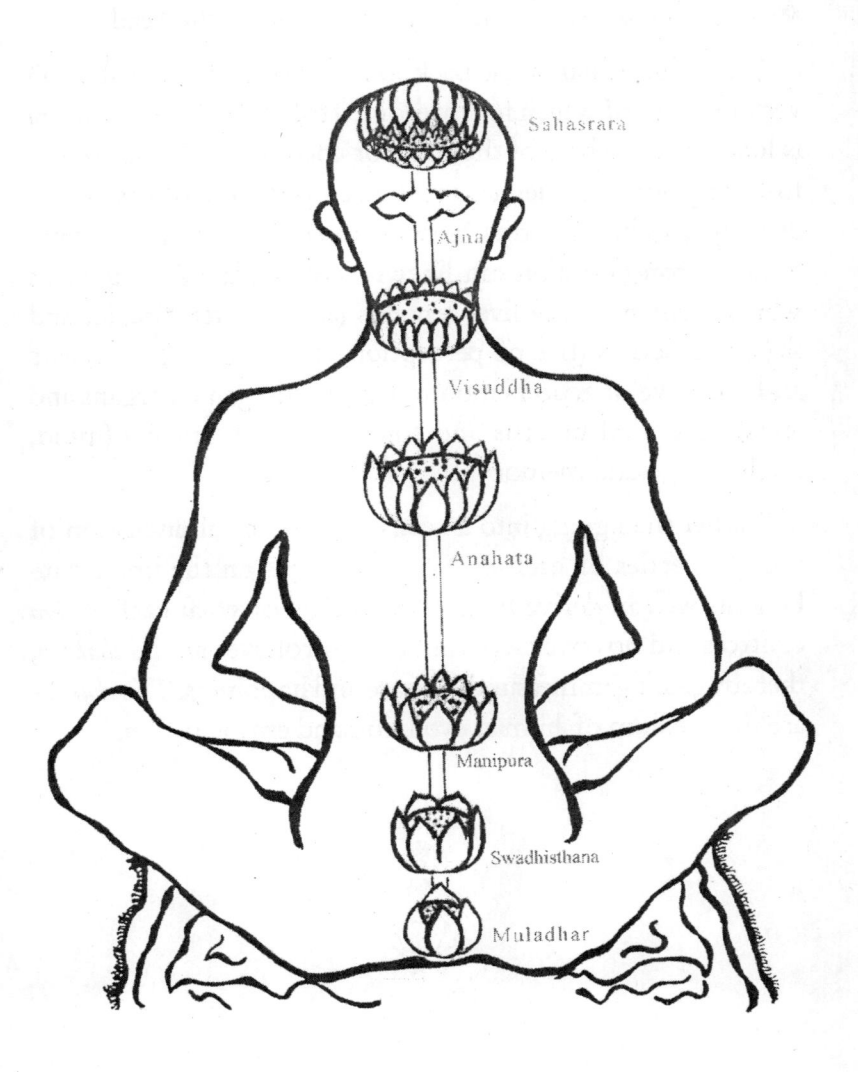

THE SEVEN CHAKRAS

- *Ajna chakra* or soul centre close to the pituitary gland.
- *Sahasrara chakra,* crown centre at the top of the head.

The spinal canal or the backbone is formed by a total of 33 vertebrae out of which four are joined together. The *Muladhara* is located at the base of the spine or coccyx where four bones fuse together with the sacrum. The 24 vertebrae represent the 24 principles in the body. One who can control these vertebrae with his concentration can likewise control the 24 principles which consist of the five elements (earth, water, fire, air and sky), ten senses (five of perception - tongue, skin, nose, ears and eyes; five of action - mouth, legs, hands, genital organs and anus), five vital breaths and four inner instruments (mind, intellect, ego and memory).

Rather than going into an elaborate technical discussion of the properties of each *chakra*, I will focus on the immediate benefits we can derive from a knowledge of what each *chakra* controls and how we can maintain control over all the *chakra*s, thereby gaining immeasurable peace and happiness. The *chakra*s are the medium of human evolution and emancipation.

MULADHARA CHAKRA

Muladhara chakra: at the base of the spine, is ruled by the earth element, has strong impact on our material accomplishments through possession of wealth, prosperity, fame, success, popularity and power. Our longings for these things keep us anchored here in the lowest centre

Location: Base of the spine
Number of petals: Four
Element: Earth
Color: Golden yellow
Presiding Deity: Ganesha
Quality of Nature (Guna): Tamas (Inertia)
Seed syllable: Lam

Sense organs:	Nose (organ of smell), anus (organ of excretion)
Taste:	Sweet
Benefits due to Concentration:	Physical comfort, External beauty, Money and Happiness of a lower grade.
Name of the Fire:	Dakshinagni (Fire in the South)
Vrittis (Tendencies):	Pleasure through material possessions, Desire to possess, Charity prompted by ego and vanity; and Greed.
Loka (Plane of existence):	Bhuh
Vital breath:	apana (helps for excretion)
Glands:	Gonads
Virtue:	Shama (Control of the Mind)
Zodiac:	Aquarius and Leo
Ruling Planet:	Saturn

The *Muladhara chakra*, which is located at the base of the spine, is one of the most powerful centres, since it represents the last confluence of three holy rivers – or three pranic channels passing through the spine. We need to take a dip in these rivers, that is, concentrate at this centre, before we begin our spiritual journey upwards. In Sanskrit, *Mula* means root, and *adhara* means support or base. Whether within the body or in the outside world, we need a foundation, which is represented by the earth or *mula*. The base of the spine contains the earth element. This centre is also called the money centre because it is associated with the material world.

Acquiring Wealth

In order to acquire anything in this world, we need money. We need money for our education, to buy a house or a car or in case of a wedding. We require money energy also for our simplest daily food and for some primary needs even if reduced to the minimum. The *Muladhara* is the *chakra* representing money, but we must understand what is intended by 'money'. The term money, in this particular case, doesn't mean currency or coins, but the physical resources or the buying capacity of a person. To be able to specify how much money we exactly need, we have to be either highly spiritual or complete lunatics.

Everyone says they want money, but no one is ever capable of specifying how much. Our needs and their complementary greed keep on increasing. The *Muladhara* takes up most of our time, life and energy. We spend the majority of our waking moments earning money to either pay off loans from the past, to enjoy ourselves in the present or to save up for the future. Our existence is ruled by this centre. In comparison other activities such as eating, sleeping, creative work, even building a relationship, in comparison, take up much less time.

We need to regulate this center and carefully analyze our effective physical and financial needs. Material wealth should be like a pair of shoes that fit us perfectly, nor too big nor too small. If the shoes are small they hurt and if they are too big they are uncomfortable.

The development of the *Muladhara chakra* enhances our material prosperity by strengthening our earning potential. Assets, fame, luxuries and power are all benefits of a highly developed *Muladhara chakra*. While focusing on the *Muladhara*, this *chakra* opens us up to the abundance of the Universe and makes us grateful recipients, as mere prosperity or fame without adequate understanding of their purpose can be extremely detrimental if not even outright dangerous. There are many examples of people who have not been able to handle the sudden influx of fame and money, and who have turned either to drugs or alcohol for support. Elvis Presley, Marilyn Monroe, and many other celebrities and millionaires ended their lives in despair despite being blessed with remarkable wealth.

Those who are engaged in regular meditation practices centered on the highest goal of self meditation, succeed in opening the *chakra*s in a steady and informed way and gain steadiness of mind which makes the vagaries of affluence seem quite irrelevant. Such people are able to handle the material benefits of the *Muladhara* without losing their balance and know how to use the wealth and power gained to benefit all of mankind, further than themselves. Their serene and meditative outlook helps them focus on the good of humanity and dissipates their selfish interests. To such people material wealth is nothing more than a reflection of the abundance of the earth and gold, unless useful for a higher purpose, is little more than dust to them. A story from the *Puranas* well illustrates this truth.

Gold or Dust?

A husband and his wife, a very spiritual couple, were walking along a country road. On the way the husband saw a gold coin. Assuming that his wife could be tempted by the gold if she saw it, he quickly covered it by kicking some dust over the gold coin with his shoe. His wife saw him scuffling and asked what he was hiding. So the husband had to confess that he had covered a gold coin with dust, so it would not become a source of temptation for her. The wife, who was much more spiritually advanced than her husband, replied: "Do you still see a difference between gold and dust? They are both the same to me."

It is only when we can cultivate this kind of attitude that we can be free from the insatiable craving for more and more wealth. Yes, wealth is necessary, but like the earth, it is only a foundation for greater activities, nothing more.

Ganesha

Ganesha is the presiding deity of the *Muladhara chakra*. In the Indian spiritual tradition, Ganesha is worshipped for success before any important undertaking. In Hindu religion the form of Ganesha or the form of any deity is not only attractive and fascinating, but has a profound symbolic meaning. The rational mind is often unable to comprehend the subtle spiritual truths and the practical teachings that lie behind these images. Ganesha is depicted as having a human body with an elephant's head, a strange combination indeed, but the underlying meaning for this symbolic image is very interesting and hints to great truths. An elephant has big ears, a long trunk and very small eyes if compared to the rest of its body. The elephant's long trunk symbolizes the importance of breath control, while its huge, flappy ears represent the receptive attitude necessary to absorb valuable knowledge and the small eyes indicate keen observation. Let's see how these three factors relate to our own spiritual journey.

Receiving Knowledge

The big ears highlight the need to listen more. To achieve real success in life, we need to talk much less and listen a lot more, but there is a further step required, as whatever one imbibes by listening more, can only be termed as learning, but true wisdom dawns only when actual Truth is revealed and experienced in deep meditation.

Once we have stilled the mind, we need to listen to the divine sound, the continuous primeval vibration that resounds in the outer and inner universe. All our life we have been suffocating this vital sound with the constant rattling noise of worldly life, deafening music and even boisterous thoughts, but the divine sound has always been there waiting to be heard.

We need to ponder daily the ancient scriptures and possibly have them explained directly from a teacher, a realized Master, as spiritual truths cannot be properly imbibed by reading any book at random. Every day new volumes are printed describing all kinds of transcendental experiences. Most people regard the spiritual arena as an open forum to show off their own fantasies, as they perceive it like a place without rules, where one is free to indulge in one's own private reveries.

It is true that spiritual experiences are highly personal and may differ from one person to another, however, choosing the spiritual path involves a lot of discrimination, inner understanding and determined effort. Self-realization is the ultimate goal for everyone, but it is not an easy task, although the benefits far outweigh any effort required. We cannot expect immediate results nor seek shortcuts avoiding efforts. We should choose the scriptural text that most appeals to us and meditate over one verse at a time, brooding over its deepest meanings, so that the most profound inner truths may be revealed to us. All the ancient scriptures, the *Bible*, the *Gita*, the *Koran* or the *Torah* contain the distilled wisdom of the ages.

Energizing the Body

Ganesha's long trunk represents the importance of deep breathing. The modern world has only recently discovered the immense benefits to the entire physical and mental health spectrum of deep, rhythmic breathing. The fitness industry has been revolutionized by this "new discovery" and hundreds of new methods are being taught which incorporate this technique rather than strenuous physical exercises to keep the body and mind fit and active, yet in reality, this had already been discovered by the ancient sages of all religions thousands of years ago. Every scientific meditation technique incorporates this deep breathing, which floods the brain and the blood cells with the necessary oxygen and gives instant relaxation to the mind. Every serious spiritual aspirant needs to incorporate deep breathing into his or her daily routine.

Observing the Mind

Ganesha's small eyes represent keen, precise observation. We need to focus our attention on the workings of our own mind, watch how it runs here and there, never immobile, a continuous flow of unceasing thoughts. Our goal is to eventually still that turbulent flow of thoughts, focussing our mind, first on fewer and fewer thoughts till we are able to keep our attention concentrated on only one thought. In meditation, we try to still the mind, bringing it from one thought to the complete cessation of all thoughts. It is only in absolute silence that we can hear the divine sound, enabling us to take control of this *chakra* and then to move on to the higher centres.

Two sense organs are regulated by the *Muladhara chakra*, the anus and the nose; both are associated with smell; which is the quality of the earth element. These two sense organs are regulated through the simple technique of concentrating in this centre.

SWADHISTHANA CHAKRA

This Chakra is also known as the sexual centre: situated in the spine, behind the genital organs, it is ruled by water and has a strong hold over our emotions and passions. This centre often demands a good part of our time and energy.

Location: *Sacral region*
Number of petals: *Six*
Element: *Water*
Colour: *Colourless*
Presiding Deity: *Durga*
Quality of Nature (Guna): *Rajas (Activity)*
Seed syllable: *Vam*

THE UNIVERSE WITHIN

Sense organs:	*Tongue and genitals*
Taste:	*Astringent*
Benefits due to Concentration:	*Control over water element and Fulfillment of material desires.*
Name of the Fire:	*Grihapati agni (household fire)*
Vrittis (Tendencies):	*Doubt, Disobedience, Cruelty, Destructive desire, Illusive pleasure and Involvement.*
Loka (Plane of Existence):	*Bhuva*
Vital breath:	*Apana (helps for excretion and ejaculation)*
Gland:	*Gonad*
Virtue:	*Dama (Control of Senses)*
Zodiac:	*Pisces and Virgo*
Ruling Planet:	*Jupiter*

The *Swadhisthana chakra* is located in the spine in the sacral region behind the genital organs. *Swadhisthana* in Sanskrit means the place where the mind is established for a long time. After the *Muladhara*, this is the centre, which demands most of our time and energy. The water element predominates in this region and it is subtler than the earth element. While earth has a shape, size and independent existence, water needs a container and takes the shape of the container. In each *chakra*, there is a symbol.

In the *Swadhisthana* the symbol is of two triangles like those found in the Jewish Star of David. One triangle represents the female aspect and the other represents the male aspect. In Hinduism, God or the Absolute Brahman is considered to have no gender. Without gender, no creation is possible. When the Absolute divides into male and female aspects, then we have creation. Shakti, the female aspect, is a must for creation and therefore the presiding deity of the second centre is Durga which is another name for Shakti.

Sex and Food

The two sense organs ruled by this centre are the tongue and the genitals. Moderation in eating and in sexual activity, avoiding the pitfalls of gluttony and sexual overindulgence, is one of the prime requisites in attaining lasting peace and tranquility. This is not to say that, unless one lives the austere life of a monk, subsisting on roots and tubers and practicing strict celibacy, one cannot attain realization. In fact, the overly zealous practice of austerities can be as much of a handicap as overindulgence in sensual pleasures. Those who eat too much, as well as those who continually fast, cannot progress spiritually. The life of Buddha is a perfect example.

Buddha's Realization

Prince Gautama left behind all his worldly possessions and pleasures in the pursuit of truth. He gave up his kingdom, his family and the luxurious life he knew. With great determination he decided to sit and meditate until he achieved self-knowledge, declaring: "I will sit here. Let the body dry up. Let my skin, flesh, and bones be destroyed. I will be self-realized" (*Buddha Charita*).

He sat for forty days without food or drink, but when later on he related what he had experienced during those forty days to his disciple, Ananda he also specified: "I was so weak, I was hardly able to move my limbs. When I touched my stomach, I could feel my backbone. My scalp was so dry that the hair was falling off. My eyes had receded deep inside my skull and those who saw me thought that I was a ghost" (*Buddha Charita of Ashvaghosh*)

After this experience Gautama Buddha realized the folly of his extreme measures, since he had discovered he could not concentrate in such physical agony. He accepted the food offered by Sujata, a noble lady of a nearby village and slowly came back to normal. Buddhism, therefore, advocates the middle way, which avoids all sorts of extremes, in order to gain self-knowledge.

Not Enough Salt

For meditation and spiritual progress, we need moderation in food as well as in sexual enjoyment. Spiritual seekers must be able to control the mind and make it listen to new instructions. A small example: if there is a little less salt in the food, instead of over reacting, we need to instruct the mind to accept it.

Ten years ago I visited a Shiva temple near Cuttack in Orissa. After the worship, when the pandits presented me with the consecrated offering on a banana leaf, they asked the *brahmacharis* to bring me some salt. I objected that I did not need any extra salt. The pandit replied that the food did not contain any salt at all. When I asked why, he explained that the king who had constructed the temple centuries ago had arranged for all provisions and supplies for the temple, but left out any provision for salt. Since that time, in the temple, it had become a tradition to cook all the offerings without any salt. After I heard the story, I answered: "If Lord Shiva Himself has been accepting the food offered here for centuries without salt, I can surely manage for one day without it."

It is essential to have some control over the tongue. One way of practicing control over the tongue is to give up our favorite food for a while. If we are addicted to sweets, we should try giving up sweets for a certain period of time. If we have a strong habit of drinking coffee or tea, we might try foregoing it for a few days. In this way we can gradually gain control over the tongue.

The Seduction of Taste

In our search for pleasure, we go on abusing the seven centers, which have been given to us for our own personal growth and realization. The digestive fire burns within us to turn nutritious healthy food into fuel for the body and yet, in our craving for taste, we dump unwholesome, greasy, unhealthy, chemical laden foods and beverages in our bodies. If we think about it, the taste sensation hardly lasts a few seconds, the first two or three bites are all we actually taste and, after that, we might as well be eating tasteless cardboard. Yet we go on eating automatically, pouring food down our throats unaware of its taste. There are lessons in all we do and everything we experience, so we should try and understand what we are to learn from this particular one. Life is full of illusion; the web of illusion is sheer light, delicate and feeble, it sparkles with a thousand rays of enticement and promises. It pulls us in so many different ways, luring us with its ephemeral quality, intangible yet palpable, promising so much yet giving so little.

Knowing What We Want

It is so rare that we stop and ask: "What is it that I want? What is it really that I am looking for?" Instead we lunge at the nearest promise of happiness, whether it is food or sex or marriage or business and, when that promise is broken or unfulfilled, we still refuse to examine ourselves, but blame the circumstances, blame the situation or our partners, unwilling to look within and perceive what it is we really and truly want. We all want uninterrupted happiness, that unending bliss which cannot be found without, but within. The sooner we learn to stop seeking temporary pleasures in the world, and dwell in the permanent joy of the soul, the sooner we will reach our goal and fulfil the desire that has driven us on from the day we were born until the moment that, exhausted, we give up this weary body. So be moderate in enjoyment, as without this resolve, spiritual progress is very difficult.

Yayati's Curse

There is a beautiful story in the *Mahabharata* about a king called Yayati who had married Devayani, the daughter of a Brahmin Sage called Shukra. Devayani brought with her as a maidservant a princess called Sarmishtha. In the course of time, King Yayati fell in love with his wife's beautiful maidservant and, eventually, even had children from her. Devayani's father, became enraged with Yayati's conduct and cursed him with premature old age. Yayati's mind, however, still longed for sensual pleasures and was unhappy to have such an old body, so he begged his father-in-law to forgive him and withdraw his curse. The father-in-law relented, saying that if any of Yayati's sons would be willing to take the curse upon himself, then Yayati could regain his lost youth. The story goes that one of the sons of Sarmishtha, called Puru, agreed to this and the king could have his youth back which he used to continue his sense enjoyment. When he finally did reach a ripe old age with an ample and eventful life behind him, Yayati uttered a truth, which he had discovered through his life-long experience. As, despite all his sense indulgement, passion was still burning undimmed within him, he died giving this following advice to his sons and grandsons: "Children, do not believe that by indulging in sense pleasures, you can extinguish the fire of passion. In reality yielding to desire is like adding fuel to the fire. The more you indulge, the brighter it burns." Sexual desire is like smoldering fire and when this fire burns out of control, life becomes miserable. We need to use this fire in a regulated way, by disciplining the mind step by step. The sexual centre's passion and energy can be channeled toward the higher centres, where creativity and philosophy will emerge.

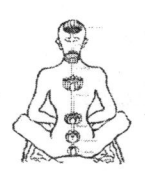

THE UNIVERSE WITHIN

MANIPURA CHAKRA

This Chakra is also known as the Navel Center: it is the food center where we derive our physical energy, beauty, lustre and vitality.

Location:	Navel region
Number of petals:	Ten
Element:	Fire
Colour:	Red
Presiding Deity:	Surya or Sun
Quality of Nature(Guna):	Rajas, Activity
Seed syllable:	Rang
Sense organs:	Eyes and feet

MANIPURA CHAKRA

Taste:	Bitter
Benefit due to Concentration:	Knowledge of the internal function of physical body, better health and physical beauty.
Name of the Fire:	Vaishwanara (digestive fire)
Vrittis (Tendencies):	Shyness, Hatred, Fear, Sleepiness, Sorrow, Idleness, Beauty, Memory, Prosperity and Vitality.
Loka (Plane of Existence):	Suva
Vital breath:	Samana (helps for digestion and assimilation)
Glands:	Liver, Spleen and Pancreas.
Virtue:	Uparati (urdhvarati- upward journey/ evolution)
Zodiac:	Aries and Libra
Ruling Planet:	Mars

The *Manipura chakra* or the navel centre is located behind the navel in the spine of the human body. *Manipura* in Sanskrit means jewel centre. The presiding deity is *Surya*, the sun. The sun is the ultimate source of all activities and the primary cause of life on this planet. Just as the moon shines reflecting the sun's light and has a strong influence on the mind, also food which is directly affected by sunlight, has a strong influence on the mind. This *chakra* is otherwise referred to as the food centre.

People chant *mantras* like the *Gayatri* to attract the divine illumination of the sun. By concentrating on this centre and experiencing our inner source of energy, we can also obtain divine illumination for the body and mind.

The two sense organs controlled by this centre are the eyes and the feet. Since we are born our eyes are constantly active in sensory perception. Even as children human beings immediately become attached to names and forms and smile only at familiar faces, but burst into tears when confronted with a stranger. As grown ups, all human beings mistakenly tend to make judgments based solely on appearance, always seeking out only what pleases the eye.

The beauty industry thrives on this tendency, luring us to spend small fortunes on products that will make us more attractive in the eyes of others. Today the fashion industry, the fitness industry, the entertainment and tourist industry and almost every consumer based market in the world, depend on our slavery to the sense of sight. If, instead of being attached to names and forms, we were able to see the beauty of God in everything, all these multi-million dollar industries, as well as their dire by-products such as eating disorders and depression, would disappear overnight.

It has been scientifically observed that the eyes of a restless person or a mentally depressed person move very quickly and blink frequently. In the desperate urge to drink in more and more stimuli, we become confused and mentally anxious. The eyes of those who meditate blink less. They have a detached look. By gradually controlling the mind through meditation and deep breathing, we are able to gain detachment from the sights which surround us, thereby avoiding sensory overload.

By focusing on the navel centre during meditation we can gain control over our restlessness and direct our vision inward to the immense inner splendor and start understanding the profound spiritual truths one may find within. Then, when we do look at the world again, we are able to perceive the magnificence of God's creation, see the essential inner beauty in all those who surround us and appreciate even the situations that confront us. We soon learn to love our surroundings without becoming excessively attached, so that we may enjoy the world without being enslaved by the world.

Our feet lead us towards many different directions. The urge to move here and there, never being able to sit still, is purely a physical reflection of the mind's inability to focus and remain calm and still in one place. People travel all over the globe on the mistaken assumption that traveling thousands of miles will somehow make them happier.

Some people cannot last in one job for very long, they need change, excitement, diversity and are soon bored with their current environment. They drift from job to job, from town to town, continually seeking an elusive fulfillment. On a more basic level, we may have noticed how many people are simply unable to sit still. Their legs are moving even when they sit on a chair, they tap their feet or always shake their legs in a nervous need for motion. Meditation enhances the ability to sit still in one position for an extended period of time. When the mind is tranquil, so is the body.

Meditating on the *Manipura* develops our ability to remain tranquil and peaceful, to direct our every movement for a useful purpose. Rather than looking here and there to seek satisfaction, yet finding it nowhere, by meditating in the Manipura chakra, we are able to progress thanks to the concentration and energy one can gain from this centre.

Food and Temptation

There is a story in the Hindu epic, the Ramayana, which illustrates the immense power food has on the mind and how food can lead man to temptation. This story proves that the old adage 'the way to a man's heart is through his stomach' to be true.

There was once a great sage called Vibhandaka, who underwent strict austerities and engaged himself in deep meditation in order to achieve realization. One day, tempted by the beauty of a celestial nymph, he lost his concentration and self-control and ran after her. They had a child, whom he named Rushyasrunga. Having learned from bitter experience that hidden desires may cause spiritual downfalls, he decided to raise his son far away from the attractions of the world. Rushyasrunga grew up in the forests under the strict guidance of his father. He was always engaged in meditation, study and other spiritual practices and therefore was brought up totally unaware of life's luxuries, delicious food, alcohol or beautiful women.

MANIPURA CHAKRA

Meanwhile, in a nearby kingdom, there was a severe drought, so the distressed king consulted his advisors who predicted that there would be rain if the young saint Rushyasrunga , who possessed great spiritual wealth and purity, entered the kingdom. However no one knew how to tempt him and take him away from the strict supervision of his father. The problem was solved when a beautiful courtesan named Jarata offered to undertake the task. She asked the king for a luxurious boat lavishly equipped with a great variety of delicious foods and beautiful damsels dressed in their finest clothes and jewellery. Docking at a distance, she waited for Rushyasrunga's father to leave and then approached the young saint. The stunningly beautiful women fed him delicacies he had never tasted before and returned each day, bringing him new and tasty dishes to tempt his palate. Having eaten this rich food, the young man gradually developed body consciousness and then attachment to his body. One day, the courtesan invited him on their boat and, once he was aboard, they set sail for the kingdom. The moment Rushyasrunga set foot on the ground, rain came pouring down, ending the terrible drought. The king asked the young saint's forgiveness for the ruse and offered him his daughter in marriage.

The old sage Vibhandaka accepted the inevitable, realizing once again that, however far we may run from temptation, unless we cultivate inner strength, we cannot resist the lure of the senses. Food is one of the strongest of these lures, tempting us like the bait tempts the fish, while it dangerously hides an iron hook.

We Eat Food and Food Eats Us

Both the eyes and the feet are controlled by the *Manipura chakra*, which is the digestive centre. Therefore the food we eat has a specific effect on our tranquility as, though the majority is excreted and some parts nourish the body, the subtle part influences the mind. If, for example, we eat a lot of meat or yogurt, our mind will be dull and lethargic, since most of our energy is used in digesting their heavy protein content. On the other hand, if we drink too much coffee or other caffeine-filled drinks, our mind will become nervous and agitated.

Not only the type of food we eat influences our mind, but also the way it is cooked. This is why, in ancient times, sages used to warn seekers that one had to take care of the cleanliness of the pots and dishes, the freshness of the ingredients and, at the same time be particularly careful about the person preparing the food. They firmly believed that the emotions of those who cooked the food seeped into the food itself and that the consumer could be affected by the cook's thoughts and feelings of anger, sadness or joy. In this age of fast food and dining out, such a careful approach is next to impossible as, although many more people are turning to vegetarianism for fear of contamination as well as the influx of hormones released by frightened animals at the time of their death, eating out is still an integral part of today's modern man's life. Even if one is a pure vegetarian, one must also be careful about the quality and the quantity of the food one eats. The way people earn money, how they use it and their general lifestyle have a strong impact on the mind, so one should also be cautious where and from whom the food is being bought and where one is taking food.

The Deluded Saint

There was a wandering monk who absolutely had no attachment for belongings and, as he was always traveling, he always accepted indiscriminately the hospitality of those who invited him. Once he stayed for two consecutive days in a very rich man's house. On the second day, at midnight, he was awakened by the jingling sound of a bell. On waking up and investigating he found that it came from a small bell attached to the neck of a cow which was in the yard. He thought it would be nice to have that bell to use in his worship. The thought became so overpowering that he went out into the yard, stole the bell and, after having hidden it in his bag, sat down to meditate. His mind was so agitated and restless that at first he could not concentrate, but as he tried harder, he became focused and realized what he had done. He was ashamed and surprised for having stooped to stealing, therefore he tried to understand how it could have happened. As he searched for an answer that could possibly explain this unprecedented, strange behaviour of his, it became apparent to him that it might have been due to the effect of the food he had eaten. He returned the bell to its place and the next morning, as he was leaving, he called the host aside and asked him by what means he earned his money. The rich man remained silent for some time, but then confessed that his means to acquire money were not honest or respectable. From that day onwards, the monk resolved to give up eating food in strangers' houses, as he had personally experienced how food bought with funds, which are not honestly acquired, has negative effects on the mind.

Food and mind are causally connected. Food can make the mind calm and tranquil or restless and agitated. Food is not only a means to nourish the body, but it may also promote calmness of mind and inner peace. When I say food eats us, I am referring to the various diseases caused by wrong food consumption, contaminated food, unwholesome foods or overeating, which in turn eat away our health. While some foods cause cancer, others cause high cholesterol and heart attacks. Every day, the list of unhealthy foods becomes longer. It is advisable to take simple and wholesome food and to offer it to God before we eat. The tradition of praying before meals does not limit itself to simply thanking God for the food He has provided; but it also entails offering our food to God asking Him to accept it, thus making it safe for consumption, assimilation and for an overall benefit to our health.

The Fire of Illumination and Elimination

Fire has two qualities. It is a source of illumination and it provides light to others, it burns resulting in heat and energy, but it can also eliminate and destroy things. The navel center is symbolically the place of food and drink. One may obtain brilliance in mind and body from the digestive fire and, at the same time, through the process of combustion and digestion, one eliminates waste matter from the body. In Hinduism, the digestive fire is considered to be extremely sacred, and the *Bhagavad Gita* (15/14) states that God Himself burns as the fire in the navel centre, so what we eat is nothing more than an offering to Him. If we eat in that spirit, accepting food as a gift from God, choosing healthy and nutritious food, prepared in a clean and tranquil environment, and offering it back to the Giver, then we can come to no harm. By developing the navel centre, we can enjoy the food we eat and its effect on us will be wholly beneficial.

The Creative Knot

The *Muladhara*, *Swadhisthana* and *Manipura chakras* together make up what is called the *Brahmagranthi* or the creative knot, as all creative activities are accelerated through these three *chakras*. This knot, on the other hand, is also a barrier for one's spiritual evolution, so one has to penetrate or cut this knot in order to evolve and go higher spiritually. To do this one needs four things: a strong desire, firm determination, immense patience, and sustained self-effort. If our desire for spiritual evolution is strong enough, then nothing can stop us.

If we analyze a day's activity we may realize how much time we spend on each *chakra*. We need to strive for balance in the *chakras*, neither ignoring them completely nor spending inordinate amounts of time on any single one.

While trying to evolve, we sometimes come across failure. At this point, many people loose their patience and decide that whatever method they are trying is not for them, so proceed seeking and trying other different techniques. This is a typical disease of the modern mind. We should have the patience to persevere in our efforts and, eventually, we will be successful. Keeping the ultimate goal in sight is extremely important and determines the benefits we gain from our endeavours in spiritual evolution.

The Inner Pilgrimage

People go on vacation to striking seaside resorts or to secluded mountain resorts spending exaggerate amounts of money, take time off from work and leave their homes, in the hope to be able to relax and enjoy themselves, but then, eventually, end up by indulging only in strenuous activities like mountain climbing, water skiing or hiking and when their holiday is over, they are more exhausted than when they left. Even on weekends, people fill their itineraries with activities to enjoy themselves and, the next Monday morning, they return to work dog-tired, only just able to function.

In India, until recently, people used to take time off for pilgrimages rather than holidays. Even nowadays, including people who cannot afford it, save money and take time off only to go and visit holy shrines like Tirupati, Puri or Kedarnath in the Himalayas. In India, shrines and temples are usually either close to the sea, on riverbanks or high up some far away mountain top. A trip to places like Kedarnath or Amarnath, on the highest Himalayan peaks, is quite a strenuous one and it involves a lot of climbing, but at the end of the climb, pilgrims are rewarded and re-energized by the vision of the temple Deity and the holy vibrations of the sacred place.

So, whether one calls it a holiday or a pilgrimage, the process is the same, but the result is entirely poles apart. While tourists come home tired after having spent tons of money to enjoy an instant thrill that quickly fades away, pilgrims return to their homes with rejuvenated vigor, a peaceful mind and the satisfaction of having attained their goal.

MANIPURA CHAKRA

Only if the goal is fixed will we progress on the path of liberation. The spiritual path is a continuous journey to which we can stick to only if we have a fixed purpose, immense patience and unrelenting effort. After having conquered the three lower centres, we have to strive more, as we need some further concentration in order to penetrate the knot and proceed upwards. In meditation, when we fix our attention and go from the *Muladhara* to the *Swadhisthana* and then to the *Manipura Chakra*, we gradually gain control over the senses and go past all three to the *Anahata Chakra* or heart centre. While concentrating in these centres, one experiences spiritual energy and the unfolding play of divine consciousness.

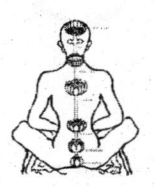

ANAHATA CHAKRA

The Heart Centre: The heart centre is the air centre. It is the emotional centre, where all our feelings, our passions, our loves and hates, likes and dislikes, which the scriptures declare as pairs of opposites arise.

Location: *Heart or dorsal region*
Number of petals: *Twelve*
Element: *Air*
Colour: *Smoky*
Presiding Deity: *Vishnu*

ANAHATA CHAKRA

Quality of Nature (Guna):	*Sattva and Rajas (Calmness and Activity)*
Seed syllable:	*Yam*
Sense organs:	*Skin (organ of touch) and Hands (organ of work)*
Taste:	*Acidic*
Benefits due to Concentration:	*Emotional development, Material gain and Material knowledge.*
Name of Fire:	*Ahavaneya (Fire of Love)*
Vrittis (Tendencies):	*Desire, Depressive thoughts, Endeavour, Possessive attitude, Arrogance, Mourning, Discrimination, Ego, Greed, Hypocrisy, Argumentativeness and Repentance.*
Loka (Plane of Existence):	*Maha*
Vital Breath:	*Prana (helps to maintain life)*
Gland:	*Thymus*
Virtues:	*Shraddha (Faith in the scriptures and teacher)*
Zodiac:	*Taurus and Scorpion*
Ruling Planet:	*Venus*

The *Anahata chakra*, or heart centre, is located in the spinal region of the human body, behind the middle of the chest. It contains vital energy.

Air is the vital life energy. Air is the symbol of stillness. The still air outside is a symbol of the still air inside which is the same vital life energy referred to as *prana* in Hindu scriptures. When the air becomes restless outside, it blows as a breeze or a wind and when air moves inside the body, it manifests as the breath. When the wind outside becomes strong, it can take the form of a cyclone or a hurricane, causing a natural disaster. Likewise, when our breath becomes fast and strong, it results in the damaging emotions of anger, passion, depression, and tension.

Through breath control and self-control, *Yogis* regulate their life energy and are able to tread the path of inner peace and joy. While prana or life energy can be classified into different types, each responsible for a diverse number of activities, the heart remains the place of the main vital life force, which regulates the breath.

The Sons of Vayu

Breath control is self-control, breath mastery is self-mastery and breathlessness is the state of realization. Through breath control, *Yogis* are able to control their inner universe, which in turn brings control over the outer universe. Through breath control one attains immense mental and physical strength. The heart centre is the controlling and regulating chamber.

In Hindu mythology, *Vayu* is the God of Air. *Vayu*'s two sons are said to be mythical heroes. One is Hanuman, the monkey god who, possessing superhuman strength, performed incredible feats in the *Ramayana*. The other hero is Bhima, the immensely powerful *Pandava* who, in the *Mahabharata* epic, single-handedly killed the hundred *Kauravas* who represented evil and animosity. By controlling the breath and thereby controlling the mind, these two sons of Vayu became invincible.

Life is preserved in the body through breath. All the other centres are only sporadically used, but even when the body is resting, the heart centre preserves life through constant breath circulation, the unique life energy.

Emotional Disorders

The heart centre controls our emotions. Most of us are ruled by emotions. Our loves are deep and our agonies are devastating. Too rapidly do we become attached in our relationships and just as quickly do we become bored and detach. Our moods swing like a pendulum from wildly happy to dramatically miserable and desperate. Anger is an emotion we have great difficulty in controlling. It bursts forth in harsh, cruel words that, a few minutes later, we would give anything to take back. Despite our own moods, we are all extremely susceptible, unable to bear the slightest criticism, resenting it as a wound to the very soul. The heart, which should be a place of love, has become a place of anger, ego and pride.

In recent times, emotional problems have become rampant. Mood disorders, stress related disorders, depression, anxiety, suicides among adults and teens alike, have become dramatically prevalent in today's world. The pace of modern society, the stress of any work place, the loneliness and isolation of urban life and the widespread disintegration of the family unit have all been cited as the leading factors of this increased emotional turmoil. Whatever caused pain, anger or depression, there is only one cure. That is to achieve a balanced emotional state in which neither pain nor pleasure can disturb the inner calm and tranquility of our minds.

Universal Love

The heart centre can be the source of either immense emotional satisfaction or intense emotional despair. By focusing on this *chakra* and by developing our awareness through deep meditation, we can energize this centre and turn it into a source of profound inner joy – first, by achieving the balance needed to deal with ups and downs in unwavering equanimity and, secondly, by channeling our emotions into a constructive course. Our selfish love, which is the root cause of many of our problems, will be replaced with an expansive, all-encompassing love for others. All of us have the same basic need: to love and to be loved. By transforming and turning the selfish love we feel towards ourselves and our immediate circle into warmth and compassion for all those who share this earth with us, we will find ourselves released from the self-made prison of our emotions. At last we will be free to love wholly, without fear and without restraint. Through loving others, we love God, and that love returns to us a thousand-fold when it is given unselfishly and without ulterior motives.

How can such a state be achieved? Through the same process of relaxation, meditation and self-inquiry with which we overcome the downward pull of the other *chakra*s. Selfish emotion drags the mind downwards, burdening it with feelings that bury our spiritual energy and dissipate it in fleeting, momentary joys and sorrows. True happiness and spiritual awakening require that we expand our love to envelop the entire universe and thus gain the riches therein.

Vishnu -The Symbol of Tolerance

The presiding deity of the heart center is Vishnu. Vishnu is the maintainer, the sustainer of creation and a great symbol of tolerance.

Once, a great sage called Bhrugu went to visit Vishnu with the intention to test His tolerance. When Bhrugu arrived, Vishnu was sleeping, while his divine consort Lakshmi was massaging his feet. Bhrugu expected Vishnu to get up and greet him, as Vishnu is the omniscient god, but when he did not show any signs of recognizing his presence, Bhrugu became very angry and, as the greatest insult, kicked Vishnu on His Chest. Vishnu woke up and seeing the angry sage, He respectfully bowed to touch the sage's feet and said: "Please don't be upset. I am sorry I was sleeping and therefore did not acknowledge your arrival. Your soft feet must have been hurt by kicking my hard chest." Then Vishnu, to pacify the sage started massaging his feet with sandalwood paste.

Just as Brahma creates the universe with patience and Vishnu maintains the universe with tolerance and love, life is maintained in the body through tolerance, love and patience.

Centre of Transformation

Located in the middle of the seven *chakra*s, the *Anahata chakra* is also called the centre of transformation. When necessary, from here, the mind can go down to the lower three centres or travel upward to the super-conscious state, reaching the upper three centres. The path of spirituality requires the transformation of passion into compassion and emotion into devotion. This transformation is possible through the art of breath regulation and breath control which should be learnt under the proper guidance of a teacher. Sometimes people are transformed only temporarily and, after a while, temptation and passion again get hold of them, but through regular practice and determination, transformation becomes permanent, just as butter, once separated from milk by the churning process, cannot go back to the initial milk stage.

Being Vishnu the presiding deity, many believe that the presence of God is manifested more in this *chakra* than anywhere else in the body. Those who meditate concentrating in the heart centre develop love and devotion which should then be properly directed by ascending to the *Vishuddha chakra*.

VISHUDDHA CHAKRA

The Neck centre is the centre of creativity and of the intellect. Our best creative work, including literature, art, music, philosophy and theology emerge from the activities of this centre.

Location: The base of the throat

Number of petals: *Sixteen*

Element: *Sky*

Colour: *Smoky white*

Presiding Deity: *Shiva*

Quality of Nature (Guna): *Sattva (Tranquility)*

Seed syllable: *Sham*

Sense organs: Ears *(Organ of hearing) and Mouth (Organ of speaking)*

Taste: *Pungent*

Benefits due to Concentration: *Purification of the mind and Intense joy.*

Name of Fire: *Samidbhavana (Ritualistice fire)*

Vrittis (Tendencies): *Poison, Nectar, Happiness, Sacrifice, Calmness, Vociferation, Dynastical pride, Noble nature, Truthfulness, Forgiveness, Knowledge, Self control, Compassion, Straightforwardness, Vanity and Pride.*

Loka (Plane of Existence): *Jana*

Vital breath: *Udana (helps for evolution)*

Glands: *Thyroid and Parathyroid*

Virtues: *Titiksha (Perseverence)*

Zodiac: *Gemini and Saggitarius*

Ruling Planet: *Mercury*

The *Vishuddha Chakra* is the centre of religious and intellectual activities. The intellect can be used for material success as well as spiritual progress. Most intelligent people use their skill and talent to achieve fame and fortune, but only a few realize the intellect's potential for inner evolution and develop love, compassion, detachment and understanding. The expression of these qualities through speech and the written word, results in the development of philosophy, which is an art as well as a science that probes deeply into the meaning of life.

Concentrating in this centre seekers acquire devotional love for God. They study and listen to the scriptures, intellectualize them and practice religion. Religion is the practical aspect of philosophy. But over a period of time, religions become overly dogmatic and, as a result, fanaticism erupts, blinding their followers up to the point of forgetting their religion's true significance. Religion is a means to evolve from the lower centres to the higher ones. All the religions of the world are petals of the same lovely flower; the flower of life and, in truth, they all complement one another.

Religious intolerance

Here is a story of three different religious representatives who were traveling in an over-crowded Indian train. They were a Hindu priest, a Muslim teacher and a Christian minister. The three of them were seated on the same row of seats, in the same compartment, and as each one of them believed to be superior to the others and obviously thought his own religion was greater than any other, they were rigidly trying to keep their distance and not even looking at each other. In front of them was sitting a journalist who was amused by their behaviour and was wondering how people could become so narrow-minded and dogmatic. It was late at night and sleep was overpowering the three men. When one is on the threshold of sleep, the gross body becomes inactive, the subtle body becomes weak, and the causal body takes over. The three men started dozing and falling on each other, but would quickly check themselves and sit straight again. Finally they all fell asleep and ended up lying with the head of one touching the feet of the other. The journalist, seized the rare opportunity and with his instant Polaroid camera, took a picture of the three men. Next morning, when they got up, they quickly moved away from each other and once more tried to maintain their air of superiority. The journalist quietly showed them the photograph with a smile.

It is our body consciousness, which creates so many differences. Religions based on such differences become compartmentalized and create only division. People who meditate deeply understand the spirit behind all religions and the inner harmonious unity that links all faiths.

The cleansing and purification of the mind are the main activities of the neck centre, which is located in the spine behind the throat. According to the Vedas, there are eight holy places within the throat, the region of purity, liberation and knowledge. Hindus believe that by taking a dip in holy rivers like Ganga or Yamuna they become pure. The body undoubtedly gets cleansed and, due to the aspirant's strong belief, also the mind may result purified to a certain extent, but this is only a temporary cleansing.

A Dip in Ganga

Once a disciple asked the great saint Sri Ramakrishna Paramahamsa: "People believe that they will be totally free from sins and negative qualities by taking a dip in the river Ganga. Is it true?" Ramakrishna replied: "There is no doubt about it." The disciple argued: "My master, I have seen people daily taking dips in Ganga, yet committing the same sins again and again." Sri Ramakrishna smiled and answered: "When a person enters Ganga, all the sins do leave him because at that time he is immersed in his love for God. The sins leave his body, but patiently sit on a nearby tree or on top of a roof. When the devotee comes out of the water and he returns to his old self again, all the sins descend on his head and he starts committing again and again the very same mistakes."

If we look at our own life, we can see the same pattern emerge. We vow to reform ourselves; we make new resolutions at least once a year, we begin with great zest and spirit, but how easily we resume our bad habits, our addictions, and our faults. There is a simile in Sanskrit, *gaja snana vat*, which means 'like the bath of an elephant' and this suggestive expression is used to describe those who never drop their bad habits. An elephant takes an elaborate bath, filling its trunk with plenty of water and repeatedly pours it over its body to cleanse it thoroughly, but as soon as it emerges from the river, it rolls in mud again. Rather than bathing in external holy rivers, what the Vedas extolled was inner purification through bathing in the internal oasis of the self, located in the *Vishuddha chakra*. The eight *Vishuddha tirthas* (holy places) are described as: non-violence, truthfulness, forgiveness, compassion, knowledge, straight forwardness, purity of the Self, and liberation.

All these eight virtues are in the neck centre. When we dive into these eight holy rivers, as they are called, we will be free from the eight types of human bondage. The causes for human bondage include: shame, hatred, fear, sorrow, jealousy, pride, ego, and prejudice. All human beings are strongly bound by these eight negative qualities, which are like strong ropes keeping us tied down. By bathing or filling ourselves with the eight divine qualities, we can purify our minds and escape the state of bondage.

Nilakantha- Blue Throat

The Hindu God Shiva is the presiding deity of the throat centre. Shiva, in order to save the world, once drank a deadly poison, which was threatening to engulf the entire universe. As Shiva knew that if he swallowed the poison, he too would be destroyed, unable to swallow and unable to spew out the venom, Shiva kept it locked within his throat. His throat, which held the poison, took on a permanent blue hue, earning Shiva the name of *Nilakantha* or the one with the blue throat.

Hindu myth always contains an underlying metaphor. Here, the throat is the centre of speech, which can be extremely powerful. With our speech, we can either create a state of harmony, love and understanding or one of hatred, bitterness and pain. The throat thus has the potential to contain poison or nectar. We need to speak with understanding and love. Like Shiva, we need to contain the bitter poison and refuse to hurt others through our words.

AJNA CHAKRA

The Soul Center: or the dwelling place of the third eye is the center for spirituality, and the residence of the soul within the body.

Location: Between the eyebrows
Number of petals: Two
Element: Beyond all elements
Colour: Smoky white
Presiding Deity: Jivatma
(the individual soul)
Quality of Nature: Pure Sattva
(extreme calmness)
Seed syllables: Ham , Ksham

Benefits due to Concentration:	*Control over adverse situations and Immortality.*
Name of Fire:	*Brahmagni (Fire of Brahman)*
Vrittis (Tendencies):	*Inner peace and Inner love.*
Loka (Plane of Existence):	*Tapa*
Vital breath:	*Prana (Life-energy)*
Gland:	*Pituitary*
Virtues:	*Samadhana (Balanced nature or equanimity)*
Zodiac:	*Cancer and Capricorn*
Ruling Planets:	*Moon and Sun*

The soul centre is located between the eyebrows, two to three inches inside the brain. Below this centre lies ignorance and above lies blissful and divine knowledge. *Ajna* also means, wish, will and instruction or direction. The directions of a teacher can take us only up to the soul centre, but beyond that we have to go on our own. The journey is strictly personal, we have come alone to this world and we have to proceed to the goal by our own efforts alone. The *Ajna chakra* is also called *Kutastha*, which in Sanskrit means immovable, self-controlled, firmly established and imperishable.

The Inner Anvil

Kuta in Sanskrit means the anvil on which precious ornaments are cast. The soul is ever unchanging and unaffected by the opposites of pleasure or pain, happiness or unhappiness, just as the anvil is unaffected by the blows of the hammer and still yields such beautiful jewels. The process of meditation and self-purification can be compared to the blows of the hammer that mould gold into delicate ornaments.

Another meaning of *kutastha* is that which is hidden from our sight. Our vision is directed outwards, but the soul itself is hidden within the body waiting to be discovered. With the extrovert senses we search for happiness in the outside world while the hidden *kutastha* is the real source of peace and joy. The soul is concealed, but it is the real conscious witness to all we see, smell, hear, touch and taste. The soul is the source of all physical and mental energy.

The *kutastha* is imperishable and is also called the third eye. When we concentrate in the *Ajna chakra* we may see a white or golden coloured light, sometimes other colours may also appear due to the predominance of any of the other *chakra*s. The *Ajna chakra* is some times also referred to as *Jnana chakra* or *Ajnana chakra* – centre of knowledge and ignorance. Above this centre is the place of knowledge and below is the play of ignorance. Those who concentrate in the *Ajna chakra* acquire complete self-control. Once one is firmly established in this centre, the senses are defeated as their source of strength lies in the centres below.

The Third Eye

The *Ajna chakra* is also called third eye or *Vishuddha*. People normally have two eyes that are the eyes of duality, which allow them to identify friends and enemies, good and bad, pleasure and pain. Duality is the cause of bondage and suffering, therefore, to pursue harmony in the duality of nature is true spirituality. Jesus said: *"The eye is the light of the body. If therefore thine eye be single, thy whole body shall be full of light."* The Bhagavad Gita as well mentions that the top of the nose, in the centre of the two brows, is the place to concentrate while meditating. The right eye is the sun, the left is the moon and the third eye is fire; the fire of knowledge. The fire is known as *brahmagni*, the fire of God, the fire of purity, knowledge and illumination. One may use the third eye only while meditating.

The Pole Star

The *Ajna chakra* is also referred to as the *Dhruva chakra*. Dhruva means to be fixed or undisturbed. In Hindu mythology *Dhruva nakshatra* is the name of the pole star. In the olden days, navigators looked up to the pole star in the north to determine the direction of their voyage. Similarly, in the inner universe, one should look up to the upper part of the body for direction. When one meditates in the soul centre one sometimes sees a bluish coloured star, the pole star.

The mythological legend states that Dhruva was a young prince who had dedicated all his life to experiencing spiritual truth. Once Dhruva became very dejected and deeply hurt when his step mother humiliated him. Suniti, his real mother, consoled him and advised him to only meditate on God. The five year old boy asked his mother where and how to proceed. She instructed him to go to the forest and meditate in peace and seclusion, thus becoming her child's first *Guru*. The young child followed her advice and went to the forest. At first he was afraid of the wild animals roaming free in the forest, but he soon established himself so firmly in the omnipresence of God that he saw only God everywhere. Dhruva is believed to have become that very pole star, which is the guiding light to many spiritual seekers.

When one meditates in the soul centre one becomes free from animal propensities and negative thoughts.

The Knot of Liberation

Two out of the three knots, the creative knot; Brahmagranthi and the knot of preservation; *Vishnugranthi* are situated below the Ajna and are helpful for the creation and preservation of life. For liberation, however, one must be able to penetrate the *Rudragranthi*. Rudra is another name of Shiva. Rudra means *prana*, or the tranquil breath. Below are the forty-nine *pranas*, which by combination and permutations become multifold and bring vibrations of various types of thoughts and propensities into our life. When one meditates in the knot of liberation this knot opens gradually and one becomes released from the pull of nature, the mind is at last disentangled and will be able to climb further up. By meditating in each *chakra* one becomes free from bondage and when one, with the help of a Guru, reaches the ajna *chakra*, one is ready to enter alone in the realm of spiritual enlightenment. When *Rudragranthi*, the knot of liberation is opened, the seeker, at last, becomes emancipated.

SAHASRARA CHAKRA

Sahasrara chakra: is the entryway to the Absolute, where the soul unites the limited universe within with the unlimited universe without. This chakra is otherwise known as Brahmarandhra (the abode of Brahman) and muktidvara (windows of liberation).

Location: Crown of the head
Number of Petals: 1,000
Element: Beyond the elements
Colour: Colourless

Presiding Deity:	*The Supreme Self (Paramatma)*
Quality of Nature (Guna):	*Beyond all qualities*
Seed Syllables:	*Om*
Benefits due to Concentration:	*Wisdom/Liberation*
Name of Fire:	*Visvarupa mahanaagni (Cosmic Fire)*
Vrittis (Tendencies):	*Experience in the atom point*
Loka (Plane of Existence):	*Satya*
Vital breath:	*Vyana (omnipresent vital breath)*
Gland:	*Pineal*
Virtues:	*All virtues manifested*
Zodiac:	*Beyond the zodiac*
Planet:	*Beyond the planets*

The *Sahasrara chakra* is located in the fontanel at the top of the head. It corresponds to the soft place in the scalp, the hole in the skull of new born babies, which closes when the child is around three or four months old, leaving a very small gap still open. The *Sahasrara* is the *chakratita chakra*, the *chakra* beyond all *chakra*s. *Sahasra* means thousand and *ara* means the spoke of a wheel. It is a wheel of one thousand spokes. Why a thousand? It is a multiple of 1x10x10x10. The number one is the Supreme Soul within the body expressed in three states of existence. The first ten represent the ten directions; four sides, four corners, above and below, which cover all the existing space. The indwelling self manifested like this is the causal body. When it is expressed through the mind and breath, it is the subtle or the astral body with its ten vital breaths, and when expressed through the ten sense organs, it is the physical or gross body. The wheel of life rotates in a thousand directions (a thousand is not to be taken literally. It simply represents a multiplicity of activities).

The *Sahasrara* is also called the lotus of a thousand petals. It is the biggest lotus. Unlike the other *chakra*s, where the lotus blooms upwards, in the *Sahasrara*, the lotus blooms downwards. Modern scientists have defined this *chakra* as the energy surrounding the brain.

The *Yogis* call it the doorway to the Infinite. When one concentrates in the *Sahasrara* there is a mixture of seven colours just as when sunlight, passing through a prism, is split into seven colours. The outermost is indigo, followed by blue, green, violet, red, orange, and yellow. The innermost place is also called the *brahmarandhra*, the hole of the Absolute. Through this opening, the soul enters the body of the baby in the mother's womb and then a few months after birth this door is being closed again.

The Vast Inner Sky

When one goes into deep meditation and reaches beyond the *Ajna chakra*, one experiences the *Sahasrara* as a vast inner sky. There are stars and planets just as in the outer sky, but if one goes even higher up, beyond the stars and planets, there is only a vast sky where there is only light. In deep meditation, when one reaches great heights, one experiences the limitless, formless aspect where all lights merge into a single light.

Polarity

The earth has terrestrial magnetism. It has a north pole and a south pole. Correspondingly, the body also has a north and a south pole. We normally say north to indicate up and south to indicate down. South is the place of material activity and north is the area of spirituality and calmness. Between the northern and southern poles of the body, all activities, material, physical, emotional, religious and spiritual are possible. At the extreme end of the North Pole, when one reaches the atom point, everything dissolves and one attains realization.

Beyond Name and Form

A father took his five children to a store to buy some candies. The sweets were in the form of dissimilar animals and each of the children picked a different form: a lion, an elephant, a deer, a bird and a human figure. Each child was convinced his candy was the best of all. The first one said that the lion was the most powerful as it could eat all the other animals and even human beings. The second said the elephant was far better as it was the biggest of all and soon started a big argument. When their mother came to see what was happening she inquired about the reason for such a quarrel and the children, sustaining their reasons, explained the origin of the fight. Their mother smiled and reminded them that in reality the essence of all the candies was only sugar, that all the different candies were all just as sweet, so they had no reason to quarrel. All they had to do was to enjoy the sweetness inherent in the various forms. The five children represent the five lower centres, busy with name and form and the mother represents the sixth centre, asserting that all names and forms are only apparent and once in the mouth the candy melts leaving only sweetness and joy. In the *Sahasrara* one is free from all names and forms, totally absorbed in oneself, experiencing inner peace and happiness.

Chakra Purification

The seven *chakras* form a garland of fourteen lotuses going up and down along the spine. Dedicate this garland to God as God was the one who gave these cosmic energy centres to man. Always connect each centre with the source of energy and, when acting through any *chakra*, never forget to act in God consciousness. While meditating, when you focus your attention on each *chakra*, offer each *chakra* to God. Concentrate, purify and energize each *chakra* through your concentration, the negative propensities of each *chakra* will be removed and your mind will be pure, happy and peaceful. The *chakra* purification is also part of an intricate yogic process, which highly advanced *Yogis* do, infusing their energy in order to help the student savor supernatural experiences.

Stars and Planets

Just as the outer universe has stars and planets that are believed to influence human life, all along the spine, in the inner universe, one finds the entire zodiac. By meditating and energizing the spine, the adverse effects of the stars and planets are neutralized. People go to astrologers to know their future through astrological calculation, yet it is our inner stars and planets, the subtle zodiac present inside the spine that can be instrumental in radiating cosmic light and thus benefiting our life's endeavours.

CHAPTER 4

THE PERFECT FAMILY

Who are you, who am I? Where did we come from? Who is my father? Who is my mother? Contemplate on this again and again and be awakened from a dream.

(Sri Shankara in Bhaja Govindam)

Oh my friend, if a man has a family with patience as the father, forgiveness as the mother, continuous peace as the wife, truthfulness as the son, compassion as a sister and mind control as the brother, whose bed is the Earth, whose clothes are the infinity of space and whose food is the nectar of knowledge, where is the cause for fear?

(Vairagya Shatakam of Bhartruhari)

Let us examine, one by one, the qualities of a perfect family and let us see how we can make them our own.

Patience as the Father

To work with love without being concerned about the result is patience. Sound decisions, sound judgment, and sound thinking are all born out of patience. Those who are patient can think calmly and make the right choices. Those who are impatient are restless and, uncertain more often than not, make hasty decisions that lead to unnecessary grief. When faced with a major problem, even before we analyze the problem and understand its nature, we tend to become very agitated and depressed. If we approach each circumstance gradually and with patience, we will almost always make the right decision. Patience brings tolerance and fortitude.

Forgiveness as the Mother

Forgiveness is the source of kindness and compassion towards our fellow human beings. Like a mother, we should be able to always give and ever forgive those around us. There is an episode from the life of Buddha, which illustrates the nature of true forgiveness.

Once Buddha was sitting under a tree in a village giving a discourse. An enraged person approached him and started calling him a hypocrite and other vile names. When Buddha did not respond, he became angrier and spat on his face. Buddha quietly wiped his face and continued his discourse. Ananda, one of his disciples, asked him; "That man abused you wrongly and you did not react. Are you a stone statue?" Buddha just smiled and continued his discourse.

The person who abused him later regretted his action and went back to Buddha to apologize. As Buddha had already left, he went to the next village in search of him. Here Buddha was giving another discourse and was again sitting under a tree. The man bowed at his feet and asked for his forgiveness. Buddha, who did not even remember the incident, asked him to remind him of what had happened. When the man gave all the explanations, Buddha replied; "We are no longer in that village nor under that particular tree. Why do you still carry that memory? I have forgotten it long ago."

Like that man, most of us tend to carry around many of our past burdens, which make our present life truly miserable. Forgiveness eases our burdens. Forgiveness rids us of the hatred, the anger, the ill feelings and the resentment that we constantly tend to carry on our shoulders, but after having forgiven, we are free to aspire to greater things without the heavy load of the past tarnishing our present.

Peace as the Spouse

Peace is the state of calmness in every situation. When we are wedded to peace, there can be no conflict in our lives. People get married for steady and lasting companionship, but most end up spending very little time together and this causes unhappiness in married life. The expected happiness in marriage vanishes if the vow of companionship is not kept. For a happy relationship one must take the vow of peaceful and lifelong companionship. Under all circumstances, in sickness and in good health, in better or worse periods, in affluent or poorer moments, one should strive to always maintain peace in one's life. When there is peace in the mind, it reflects and radiates peace everywhere.

Buddha was begging for food. One day a lady was calling him names and ridiculing him because he was begging. Buddha patiently bore all her insults and did not reply. Later the lady repented for her folly and went to offer alms to him. Buddha asked, "What would happen if I did not accept your offer?" The lady replied, "I would take it back." With a very peaceful smile Buddha whispered, "If I don't accept all your previous accusations, then you surely must take them back." The lady not only regretted her misconduct, but also understood the meaning of peace. Buddha, due to his immense calmness and peace was undisturbed and was able to show the path of peace to others.

Truth as the Child

Every word we utter is our child. Every sound is born from the mouth. We give birth to every thought, word and action we perform in our life. When we realize the importance of our own creations, the impact they have on others, we should make sure every thought, word, and action is truthful and accurate both in fact as in spirit. If there is no correspondence between our thoughts, words and deeds an inner conflict will arise.

Truth in speech should be free from falsehood and be a clear statement of what exists. Truth should be expressed in such a way as not to hurt others, the way of speaking is also as important as what is spoken. To be truthful in thought, word and deed, we should have a proper understanding and speak what we think without ever hurting others' feelings. The truth you speak should also be for the good of others. Mahatma Gandhi is a shining example of how one should uphold the value of truth throughout one's life.

God is Truth. When one lives in God-conscious thoughts and in the awareness of God's presence everywhere, there cannot be any room left for falsehood in any aspect of our lives.

Compassion as the Sister

Every action of ours should reflect compassion for others.

In order to have compassion, we need to envisage ourselves in the other person's situation and analyze the issues also under their point of view and perspective. We should also strive to understand their needs and outlook. Compassion requires that we emerge from our narrow shell and expand our love and empathy to those beyond our immediate circle. We live in the world, among people of conflicting attitudes, different behavioural patterns and expectations. Live intelligently and tactfully with mental maturity and emotional balance. Compassion stems out of human nature deep understanding and mature knowledge of how relationships work. Let us be considerate and objective about others' behaviour, if we understand the circumstances and the reasons that gave origin to certain actions, it becomes easier to be more compassionate. When a child jumps on his mother's lap, even if he hurts her, his mother compassionately accepts his actions as part of a child's exuberant and playful nature.

Love gives and forgives. Selfishness gets and forgets. Jesus is the ultimate example of compassion as he prayed for the people who crucified him.

Controlled Mind as the Brother

Be the master of your own mind, not it's slave. Keep the mind under control, without letting the mind control you. The mind can be a wonderful servant, as well as an appalling master.

The human mind can be compared to a piece of cloth. To keep your clothes clean, you have to avoid sitting in a dirty place. If your surroundings are not conducive to spirituality and progress, change them, but if you have no alternative, then be present physically, but mentally detach yourself and remain inside with Divinity. Frequently wash the cloth of the mind with the water of love and practice regularly, then the mind will become like a reliable and loyal brother.

The Story of Suka

Suka was a great spiritual seeker. His father, Sage Vyasa, had encouraged him, to go to the court of King Janaka and learn from him. Janaka, before imparting any spiritual knowledge to Suka, wanted to see if he was a worthy student, so he tested him. When Suka came to see him, Janaka was surrounded by beautiful young maidens who were massaging his body. Janaka wanted to see Suka's reaction to this, but Suka showed no sign of disturbance. Janaka then sent him on a tour around his kingdom making sure every possible lure for the senses would be displayed on his way. There were plenty of riches and jewels to tempt the money centre, beautiful inviting maidens singing and dancing to attract the second centre, a variety of delicious foods to tempt the food centre and entertainment to amuse and arouse the emotions of the heart centre. When Suka returned to the palace, Janaka asked him, "What did you see on your way and what was your experience?" Suka replied, "I have seen nothing except the play of consciousness everywhere." King Janaka accepted him as a disciple, as he had proved himself to be a most apt student.

The Earth as a Bed

When a person dies he is buried beneath the earth. We use comforters, quilts and blankets to cover our body in order to be comfortable. But the blanket of the earth has always held and comforted us. The lap of the earth is the bed for all. We are born on this earth, we play on earth and again we leave our body to the earth. Wherever you sleep, whether on a comfortable bed or on the hard floor, remember it is still the earth. A beggar's body or a king's body all go to the burial ground at the end. In German the word for burial ground is 'friedhof' which means home of peace. Sleep in the lap of God with the blanket of God-consciousness and you will find peace.

Space as the Garment

The frail human body needs clothing to wear. Both the physical body and the clothes, being made from the same earth elements are of limited existence. Once we realize we are not mere human beings, but perceive ourselves as the formless infinite, what clothes could possibly cover us? The entire space is the garment of the Infinite.

Wisdom as Food

There is food for the body, food for the mind and food for the soul. Food for the body is the food we eat to sustain the physical frame. The mind can be nourished by good thoughts and the study of the scriptures. Meditation and wisdom are the food for the spirit. Knowledge gathered from external sources, when intelligently applied, leads to wisdom, to the super or cosmic conscious state. Wisdom is the real food that a *yogi* must live on. We should daily drink from the nectar of wisdom as knowledge is a great purifier and a source of energy and strength, while ignorance causes fear and makes us weak. Knowledge makes a person strong and enables him to experience truth, therefore we need self-knowledge to realize that we are not the body; we are only playing our role through the body and the *chakra*s.

If we, as individuals, were to cultivate a family with patience, forgiveness, continuous peace, truthfulness, compassion and mind control, we would surely achieve the state of absolute peace and happiness and never again have anything to fear.

The Family of Shiva

In Hinduism, Lord Shiva, otherwise known as *Yogeshwara* is a *yogi* who leads a family life of peace, love and cooperation. Shiva lives on Mount *Kailasha* with his divine consort Parvati and their two sons Ganesha and Kartikeya. Each of them represents different aspects of life. Shiva is always absorbed in meditation. Parvati is engaged in serving her husband, symbolizing love and the path of devotion. Ganesha is wisdom and Kartikeya is the symbol of strength and valour. They all have different interests and use different animals as their vehicles. Shiva rides a bull and has a snake around his neck. Parvati uses a lion while Ganesha and Kartikeya have a mouse and a peacock as their means of transportation. Though these animals are, by nature, enemies of each other, together with this family they all live in harmony.

The lesson to be learned from Shiva's family and that we can apply in our daily lives is that we have to accept the fact we all come from different backgrounds and, even if part of the same family, its members may have different minds and dissimilar goals. With cooperation and respect for each other, we can all harmoniously live together and achieve a state of meditation common to all.

Every person, who understands the meaning of an inner family and leads this type of life with love, will always be free from fear and anxiety. Fear makes a person weak. Fear of loosing happiness and fear of death make life utterly miserable. A *yogi*, who roams in the inner universe is truly fearless, and this applies to his spiritual as well as his practical life in the world.

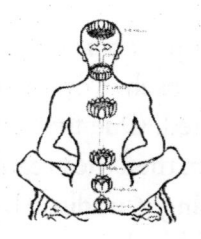

CHAPTER 5

MEDITATION: PRACTICE AND BENEFITS

Lightness, well-being, steadiness, a luminous complexion, a sweet voice, a pleasant scent and a good digestion, these, they say, are the first results of progress in meditation.

(*Svetasvetara Upanishad, II:13*)

In the olden days, people churned yogurt to obtain butter. Even if butter is latent in each drop of milk, you cannot see it unless it has been extracted. One first has to heat up the milk for the cream to come up, then the cream is turned into yogurt by culturing it and keeping it undisturbed for sometime. The last process entails churning the yogurt to separate the butter. Once the butter is separated, it will float on top of the milk, buttermilk or water and it will never mix with them again. The butter is heated to make *ghee* and this *ghee* can be a good fuel in a fire.

To innerly obtain some precious butter or ghee, the body has to be heated by the inner fire of meditation, concentrating in the region between the soul centre and the fontanel. First heat the milk of life by practicing deep, relaxed breathing. Then the cream will emerge. Every day, for a certain period of time, maintain inner silence in the mind and stillness of the body in order to convert the cream into yogurt, then continue your meditation to obtain the butter. Deeper concentration will clarify the butter and make it pure enough to burn completely in the fire, the fire of wisdom that dispels the darkness of ignorance and fear.

Where to Meditate

Many people wonder about the perfect place for spiritual practice. Once we decide to meditate, which is the best place to do so? The scriptures state that one should meditate either in the forest, in a corner of the house or within one's mind.

Let us first talk about the forest. What did retreating into a forest really entail? In ancient times, the sages retreated into a physical forest where they had to face many dangers, discomforts and wild ferocious animals. Nowadays the majority of us lives in urban areas and retreating to a forest is an obsolete, impractical and not a viable option. What did retreating in the forest actually mean? What is actually meant by 'retreating to a forest' is that we live in the shelter and solitude of our own internal forest. Also this internal forest contains the wild animals of emotion, anger and pride that any seeker must subdue through the power of meditation, so a corner in one's own home is a practical answer to today's needs. One has to choose a room or even a corner of a room that is undisturbed, uncluttered and silent where to sit each day for at least 20 minutes and meditate.

The forest and the house are physical locations. One needs time to reach one's home or to go into a forest, while to meditate internally, there is no limit of time or space. It can be done at all times, everywhere. Meditating within the mind requires the cessation of thought. We need to go inward, keeping the mind peaceful and tranquil. Whatever the surroundings, we must keep the mind always anchored in God. The mind is the best place for meditation.

Many Indian monks go to cremation grounds to meditate as it helps them gain even more sense of detachment as, just by watching end up in ashes the precious body that one normally treats with so much care, gives a brutal awakening to its temporary nature and one is forced to face the nude reality that the body is unavoidably, ultimately destined to return to the elements from which it was made.

The Proper Posture

There is a lot of confusion over the proper posture to be used in meditation. Some insist on the lotus posture, others advocate sitting cross-legged or even lye down. Any posture is appropriate as long as the body is comfortable and we are able to forget its presence. Unduly painful positions make us more aware of the body and keep us anchored in our consciousness, hindering our ability to go beyond. The *Yoga Sutra* of Patanjali recommends as the right posture for meditation a posture that keeps the body still, steady, and comfortable.

In the sixth chapter of the *Bhagavad Gita* there are very specific instructions on how and where to sit for meditation. We are asked to sit in a clean place, pure and holy. Where can this place be? If our minds are not calm and quiet, wherever we sit will not make a difference. In this body temple there is one place that is always totally serene. From the eyebrows to the top of the head is the place of utter calmness and peace. If we concentrate there, we will be able to meditate better.

MEDITATION: PRACTICE AND BENEFITS

The Proper Seat

We are instructed to sit on a grass mat over which we must spread an animal skin, preferably that of a deer or tiger and, on top of that, place a silk or cotton cloth. Some may insist on following these instructions to the letter, but the majority does not even know or understand the underlying metaphorical meaning of these instructions.

Let us analyze them carefully. *Kusa,* the Sanskrit word for grass, also means earth. In our body, the *Muladhara chakra* represents the earth. Wherever we may sit, be it on a carpet, a blanket or a grass mat we are sitting on our *Muladhara chakra* or the earth. The *asana* or seat should be non-conductor because, when one meditates, one produces much more energy in the body. Since the earth is a conductor of electricity, we should avoid sitting directly on the ground and a simple woolen blanket is more than sufficient.

If the animal skin *(ajina)* were really necessary, then we would be encouraging the killing of animals and this goes against the ahimsa or non-violent principle of Hindu philosophy. There is also another symbolic meaning for the scriptures to suggest the use of animal skin. The Sanskrit word for dead skin, *a-jina*, also means difficult to conquer. Within our body one of the most difficult places to conquer is the sexual centre. So we are being instructed to sit or go above that centre during meditation.

Finally, we have the silk or cotton cloth or *chela*. The word *chela* in Sanskrit also means fire. The centre in the body whose element is fire is the navel centre. Again we are being told to rise above the first three *chakra*s, *Muladhara, Swadhisthana* and

Manipura, in order to meditate. We need to come up to the cranium, sit there and meditate. Where to concentrate? In yoga, we are taught to concentrate on the different *chakras* and to fix our attention mostly on the top of the head.

Meditation as Worship

Lahiri Mahashaya often said "My way of worship is not the usual one. I do not need any Ganga water or flowers or utensils for my worship, nor do I burn incense or light lamps. I have forgotten who is Shiva, Kali or Durga. I am merged in myself. My way of worship is different."

There are two forms of worship. One requires a lot of preparation as one has to go to the temple or to the church, sit in front of the deity or altar, chant the *mantras* or sing. Looking, hearing, singing, burning incense are all forms of worship carried out with the help of the senses. This is external worship. The second form is that of inner worship. This worship involves closing one's eyes and seeing the light, closing one's ears and listening to the primordial sound. One only has to prepare the mind, nothing else. The spiritual journey entails nothing more than accurately preparing the mind. The gross body is born and it will die. The soul is ever pure. In between the soul and the body is the mind, which creates chaos, confusion and constant crises.

How to Meditate

In today's world there are many different meditation techniques available. Each has a unique method and tradition behind it. The important thing to realize is that all these methods have the same goal in mind. Meditation should open up the inner channels, calm and relax one's mind and body to develop the vast human potential to be divine. Material prosperity, physical and mental health, creative inspiration, intellectual prowess, increased youth and vigour, are all the benefits which result from a regular practice of any of the meditation techniques available. The goal, however, should be the search for self-knowledge, self-realization and become firmly established in one's own divine nature.

The Need for a Teacher

While the art of meditation, to some extent, can be taught through books and the technique explained and illustrated on paper, those who regularly meditate know that real spiritual practice requires the guidance of a teacher. I have been practicing a unique form of meditation throughout my life and it has given me tremendous physical, mental and spiritual benefits. I was initiated into this ancient technique by a realized Master who has guided me step by step on the path of spiritual progress. I, in turn, have initiated countless disciples into the same path, traveling around the globe teaching the technique, writing books and lecturing on the inner meanings of the most outstanding world scriptures, including not only the *Bhagavad Gita* and the *Vedas*, but also the *Bible*, the *Torah* and other holy books.

The *Kriya Yoga* meditation technique is not limited to any particular religion, rather it may be considered an effective tool to enhance whatever religion one is currently practicing or committed to. It requires no expensive equipment or physical contortions so it may be practiced both by old and young seekers.

The Basic Method

The basic method for any type of meditation is to sit for a minimum of 20 minutes a day, in complete silence, to breathe slowly and deeply from each *chakra*, concentrating intensely on that *chakra*, and to energize the entire body using the techniques taught by the teacher. After relaxing the mind and body through simple breathing and concentration exercises, one merges silently with the universe, allowing the inner voice to be heard. In that silence, we gain tremendous peace, strength and even practical answers to the questions that may be haunting us, whether they have to do with our families, our careers or our spiritual growth.

In order to learn the technique, we need to be initiated by a teacher who is qualified to purify the *chakra*s, teach the technique and guide the spiritual aspirants on their path.

Having a Road Map

It is the mind that is involved in sinful activities. The mind can go in ten different directions through the ten senses and it is restless by nature. The spiritual journey entails keeping the mind concentrated, focused and always directed toward the goal. If we gradually train the mind to go up, northwards, towards the last *chakra* at the top of the head, we will eventually reach the mountaintop of the Himalayas even if climbing physically any high peak of the Himalayan range is far easier than this inner journey.

Having a road map when you are traveling on your way to one of the Himalayan pilgrimage centres, will make the journey easier and it will allow you to reach your location with no delay. A road map gives you the confidence you are on the right path. Spiritual theory is like a road map, but merely looking at a road map does not give you the direct experience of a trip to the Himalayas. Experience comes through practice. In every breath we need to try to reach the highest peak through our own self-effort. The teacher can help, but only up to a certain extent. The teacher can give us some spiritual nourishment, but we are the ones who have to digest the food and assimilate the essence. How long can we continue to be spoon-fed? We have within ourselves the strength to overcome all our negative aspects, weaknesses and temptations.

Daily Practice

Meditating everyday is a form of disciplined self-inquiry. After we have had our lunch, we have to digest the food we have eaten, then we are hungry again. In the same way, spiritual truths, whether you absorb them reading the scriptures or gain insight through meditation, nourish us only till next session. Regular practice is extremely important; spirituality is a continuous process and not a part-time job. Someone asked a great spiritual personality, "I am meditating, but not obtaining any results." The saint answered, "You are only doing a part-time job and expecting full-time pay. How many hours of work is considered a full time job? 40 hours a week constitutes fulltime, but in spirituality we need to maintain the awakened state 24 hours a day, seven days a week." How do we maintain this state? The scriptures teach us we are to open the *Sushumna* canal in the spine in order to experience the spiritual state for ever-increasing periods of time.

The Weed-Covered Pond

There is a parable, which illustrates the necessity for constant spiritual practice and the easily camouflaged nature of spiritual endeavour.

In a village there was a big water pond. The water was covered with such thick weeds that it looked like solid ground. A stranger who did not know the peculiarity of that area, was on the point to walk across what seemed solid ground, but one of the villagers warned him about the tricky thick weeds and, to show him the danger he started pushing aside the weeds with his hands uncovering the clear water underneath. The moment the villager let go of the weeds, they moved back into place and covered up the clear crystalline water again.

This very temporary insight and then the return of illusion is exactly what happens during our spiritual practice. Even if we get some inner peace and happiness during meditation, the weeds of delusion quickly choke it up. We need to keep the pond of our mind free from all the weeds of thoughts and emotions that fill it up preventing us to have lasting peace and to experience the taste of the water of love within.

Keeping the Channel Open

Opening the *Sushumna* canal and, even more importantly, keeping it open, is not a mere physical process. The *Sushumna* is a subtle pranic canal in the spine. Practicing meditation regularly helps keep the *Sushumna* healthy and open. Whenever we experience inner peace, joy and calmness, we need to recognize it as the opening of the *Sushumna* canal. The external sign of an open *Sushumna* is the even exhalation of the breath from both nostrils. Normally, during the day, breath frequently changes from one nostril to another. It changes from right to left and from left to right in a cyclical rhythm and there are brief periods in between when it is equal in both the nostrils. Meditation is a must to keep breath flowing for a longer period of time through both nostrils, but it is still a very natural process and the unbroken regular practice is the only tool man has. Whatever path one chooses, whichever is the technique, one must practice regularly and continuously.

The Physical Benefits

If we have time, we should practice morning, noon, and evening. When we concentrate on each *chakra*, the endocrine glands function more efficiently. When we concentrate in the fontanel, the pineal gland becomes activated. Concentrating in the soul center energizes the pituitary gland. Concentration in the throat center activates the thyroid and parathyroid glands and concentration in the heart center stimulates the thymus, while in the navel centre it energizes the liver, spleen and pancreas. Regular concentration in the sacral and the coccygial centers benefits the gonads. *Chakra* meditation keeps the entire human system healthy. When we suffer from any endocrine dysfunctions, concentrating in the corresponding *chakra* helps to remedy the imbalance.

Sometimes, when the mind is too restless and we wish to meditate, it may help to focus on the picture of the form of God we love or chant His name and repeat our *mantra*, but this is only a temporary solution, a temporary remedy like taking a medicine. At the same time we should not be too attached nor to the form nor to the *mantra*. Gradually, though meditation is not imagination and it does not entail any kind of visualization, when we focus our attention on the light and sound, other experiences will come. Through concentration, our experiences become deeper and deeper, but difficult to describe in words. When we meditate for extended periods, our breathing becomes very light and we experience inner tranquility.

Through the regular practice of meditation and concentration on the *chakras*, one will experience perfect health of body, mind and spirit along with immense peace, bliss and happiness.

Joy beyond description

Each individual experience is completely personal and cannot be explained in words. It would be like feeding a mute with delicious food and then asking him to describe its taste. Although he cannot describe in words the flavour of the food he liked so much, his face will surely show his enjoyment. Similarly, even if we cannot describe what we experience in meditation, our face will show whether we are meditating or not. We are witnesses to our own experience. Our transformation is the visible result of our experience and we are the inner judges of our own progress.

MEDITATION: PRACTICE AND BENEFITS

To maintain this experience is another task. To get wealth may be easy, but to protect it is even more difficult. The only way to preserve what we have gained is to continue practicing steadily. What one has gained through scriptural study is only indirect knowledge, by practicing meditation we gain direct knowledge, which is then transformed through experience into wisdom. The study of the *chakras* helps us to understand our own activities and emotions better and it also helps us to systematically go beyond them.

The Ocean and the Waves

One who strives for one's own evolution in an integrated manner is the real spiritual seeker. Spiritual life is not for dreamers. Spiritual treasures are hard earned and are harder to preserve. The joy and bliss we may attain through our disciplined self efforts are most valuable treasures no one can ever take away from us. We are all formless, yet dreaming that we have a form. We are like the waves of the divine ocean. There are big waves and small waves, gentle waves and crashing waves, but all of them are a part of the same ocean. Our ego tells us we are separate entities while we are destined to merge with the Absolute. To experience who we are, is to experience God.

The Four Stages of Spiritual Evolution

There can be four stages of evolution:

1. When the creative knot of the *Brahmagranthi* is crossed, when we gain control over the lower three centers, we begin to see the presence of divine energy manifested everywhere.

2. When we go a little higher, we can perceive God's presence with eyes open or closed. This becomes an instinctive and natural reflex.

3. Finally when we reach the summit, we realize that we were always united with God. There is no separation and there never was.

4. When we go even beyond that, we attain the state of *Nirvikalpa*. When we attain this state, we become free from all inward attachments and live in the world like a free soul. Is our individuality lost in that state? On the contrary real individuality is gained. We discover who we are.

Churning the Ocean of Life

According to Hindu myth, the *Devas* or gods and the *Asuras* or demons decided to churn the ocean of milk in order to obtain the nectar of immortality which lay buried deep within its waters. To do this they needed a strong base on which their churning rod could rest and so they prayed to Lord Vishnu for help. He agreed to serve as the base by taking the form of a giant turtle and resting on the bottom of the ocean. As a rod they used the highest mountain, *Mandara Parvata*. Next the *Devas* and *Asuras* needed something strong enough and large enough to serve as the churning rope. They approached the giant snake *Vasuki*, who agreed to help them. The gods on one side and the demons on the other, began churning the rope in unison. Incredibly rare treasures and unbelievable fortunes began emerging from the waters. *Kamadhenu*, the cow who gave endless milk, and even

MEDITATION:
PRACTICE AND BENEFITS

Lakshmi, the goddess of wealth, rose glittering from the foaming waves. Still the *Devas* and *Asuras* went on churning, intent upon the final reward of *Amrita*, which was far superior to all these incredible appearances.

At last the *Amrita* or nectar of immortality and bliss emerged and the *Devas* and *Asuras* lined up to receive it, but soon ended up by fighting among themselves, because they were greedy and wanted to get the largest share. Once again Lord Vishnu came to their rescue by taking the form of a celestial nymph, *Mohini*, and with the trick of arousing the demons' lust, He destroyed them. In the end only the *Devas* were allowed to drink the nectar and achieve eternal bliss.

The churning of the ocean is, like most mythological Hindu stories, about the self and the quest for realization. The giant turtle represents the ability to withdraw the sense organs, for only turtles can withdraw their limbs as soon as some danger approaches. Also the senses should be withdrawn from the dangers and distractions of *Maya* or illusion. The mountain is the spine, which is used as the churning rod to churn life with the rope of breath which is represented by the snake. The mind shifts here and there, sometimes towards the *Devas* who correspond to our good propensities and sometimes towards the *Asuras* who stand for our own evil propensities. Turning first one way, then another, the mind begins spewing venom, and the churning brings forth the poison which lies at the surface: years of bad habits, thoughts, impulses begin to be churned to the surface and are released. Such a cleansing occurs in the initial stages of meditation, and the release of toxic impulses and desires can often be a painful and disturbing experience. It is only after the surface dirt is cleared, that we begin to find priceless treasures within. Wealth, prosperity, material satisfaction, comfort and luxury, fame and fortune and many powers may come to us, but like the *Devas* we should not be distracted, but continue with our effort until, at last, we obtain the nectar of bliss and self-realization. At that final moment we should be careful not to feed the demons of our evil propensities, but to strengthen our good propensities and emerge victorious.

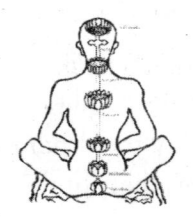

CHAPTER 6

TAPPING THE SOURCE

Arise, and awake, stop not till the goal is reached.

(Swami Vivekananda)

Throughout the preceding pages, I have stressed the importance of self-knowledge. Scientists, psychologists, and physicians through the ages have been constantly amazed and bewildered by the miracles human beings are capable of. The superhuman strength displayed by mothers who lift cars to save their children, the uncanny instincts which warn us of danger or betrayal, the unbelievable acts of heroism demonstrated by human beings in times of distress or calamity further to everyday common place miracles of kindness, creativity, scientific achievement, technological breakthroughs and spiritual love which are apparent everywhere we turn.

The Human Miracle

How are all these miracles possible? While God's universe is a phenomenon beyond description, filled with rare and stunning wonders, it is far surpassed by the constant wonders streaming forth from our own inner universe. Human beings are capable of tremendous feats, not just heroes or geniuses or artists, but ordinary human beings and each has the potential for unlimited achievement. Unfortunately, due to the fact that human beings misunderstand the God-given treasures of breath and intellect, constantly misusing them, they are not always ready to explore the manifestation of Divinity within themselves.

Hidden Treasures

Long ago, when I was a schoolboy, I read a story in a book about a father who used to be extremely hard working and sincere, but had four sons who happened to be totally lazy, irresponsible and good-for-nothing. The father, who was optimistic, never lost hope of changing his wayward sons even if they were no longer so young. When he was about to die he called his sons and told them that he had kept a hidden treasure in the barren land behind their home and that, after his death, they should search for it and share it among themselves. Shortly after this conversation the old man died. After the death of the father, the four lazy sons started to look for the hidden treasure. They dug the entire land until it was nicely tilled, but were quite disappointed when they found nothing. At first they felt desperate due to their unfulfilled expectations, but after sometime one of them suggested to sow some seeds, since it was close to monsoon and, after a few weeks, the entire field became green with plants that soon turned into a golden harvest. Looking at the crop in the field, the brothers finally understood what their father meant by "Hidden Treasure".

Also God, our Divine Father, gave us a field. The field is our body. If, we lovingly plant the seeds of good qualities in the body-soil, a hidden treasure will arise. While we sit in meditation, hidden truths will slowly be revealed to us. Having closed our eyes and shut off our senses, with our inner eye, we will perceive our divine crop, the real treasure within.

Life remains barren if not properly used, but it can give everything and in great abundance if we direct it towards the goal of life. Most of our energy lies untapped because, rather than looking towards the source, we spend our precious time searching for answers outside ourselves. Meditation is the key with which we can unlock the treasures buried deep within us, which can transform our lives from ordinary to extraordinary, attaining success in every arena of life and filling our life with love and happiness.

Dive Deep, Fly High

As in the past owning land was considered prestigious, people tried to own as much territory as possible. Soon they even crossed the seas to acquire lands on the other side of the world. Then they discovered the treasures underground and this lead to digging and mining and accumulating precious metals. Next came diving into the sea for hidden treasures. These activities of mining and diving are symbolic and associated with a special technique of breathing as the breath has to be regulated in a certain way to be able to do this. From digging and mining into the earth and diving deep into the sea we should learn that, if we want spiritual treasures, we should practice the art of breath control and self-control. The human mind is not happy with momentary gains and pleasures. It wants to dive deep and fly high to find the treasures of the soul. Remaining in the soul centre, one can go down to the lower centres of earth and water or fly high into the fontanel to tap the real source of joy and pleasure.

The Dazzling Jewel

A man was walking down the street and on his way he found a dazzling stone which seemed to be precious. He brought it to a jeweller for an estimate and since it was indeed a valuable gem, he became rich overnight. From that day onwards, while walking he was always looking down in the hope of finding another stone that would make him even richer. He was getting old and one day, as he was walking, he found another stone which was even more dazzling than the previous one. When he picked it up he realized it was just a piece of broken glass that was reflecting the brilliance of the sun. Overwhelmed he looked up to see a beautiful sun shining in the bluest of the skies. He could not recall having seen anything so beautiful in a long, long time. He threw away the piece of glass and from that day onwards, while walking, he started looking up. In life, even if sometimes we do have to look down, we should always remember to look high up into the effulgence of light.

Stop the Play of Mind

Tapping the source is possible only if we can stop the play of mind. The mind is the cause of all trouble. The mind is always restless and unless it is controlled in a regulated way, it will not be possible for us to go to the source. The mind, once regulated, trained and well directed can be a good friend, a supportive pillar in life. The mind has immense strength and the potential to overcome all life's hazards. A concentrated mind is the needed instrument to achieve the goal of self-realization.

Blissful State

We are born in bliss, live in bliss, and merge in bliss. This blissful state is inexhaustible and unending and it may be attained reaching the source in the cave of the cranium, near the fontanel, the state of perfect and infinite joy. The key to life is that within the short span of our existence, and with a limited body frame, we should experience the limitless soul and achieve enduring bliss. Arise, awake and do not stop till the goal is achieved. The Kingdom of Heaven is within. Undertake your journey with self-discipline and relentless effort, become a monarch in your own kingdom by being the architect of your life. By exploring all the *chakras* and spending a few minutes each day stilling our active minds, shutting down our overactive senses and listening quietly to the divine sound, we can tap the source within us and emerge with the unending bliss we have been searching for all our lives.

As Buddha said in the Dhammapada: "From meditation wisdom springs, without meditation wisdom declines. Knowing the two paths of progress and decline, a man should choose the path, which will increase his wisdom. Moderation in speech, control of the mind, abstention from evil actions, thus these three modes of action are purified first of all, to join the path shown by the sages."

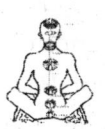

ABOUT THE AUTHOR

Paramahamsa Prajnanananda, the current head of the Kriya institutions started by Paramahamsa Hariharananda, has taken on his Master's mission of bringing the ancient secret teachings within the reach of common people who are thirsting for spiritual knowledge. Paramahamsa Prajnanananda was born in 1960 in the village of Pattamundai in Orissa, India. He has always been a sincere seeker of truth. After a childhood filled with prayer and a youth enriched by education joined with meditation, the former Triloki Dash became a caring teacher as a professor of Economics and guided and inspired many of his students spiritually.

As a college student, through an unquenchable thirst for God, he met many saints and visited many ashrams in the Himalayas, looking for a spiritual guide. While still a student, he met his master Paramahamsa Hariharananda, who initiated him into the path of Kriya Yoga. Brahmachari Triloki Dash was later initiated into the glorious path of *Sannyas* by his master, becoming Swami Prajnanananda Giri. On August 10, 1998, on his 39th birthday, the title of Paramahamsa, the highest title reserved for monks who attain the summit of realization, who are inspired and divine teachers, guides and saints, was conferred upon him by his loving and divine master Paramahamsa Hariharananda.

A truly powerful and extremely loving teacher, author and speaker on world religion, well versed in the scriptures of the East and West, he combines a divine compassion for humanity with his love for God and his mastery of complex philosophical thoughts. His vast knowledge and his oratory and intellectual skills are fully utilized in interpreting deep philosophical thoughts in the light of modern science and psychology. His metaphorical interpretation of the scriptures is very unique. Using Kriya Yoga as a reference point and an interpretative tool, Prajnanandaji manages to reveal the hidden truths contained in the most complex passages of the sacred texts in ways which make the meanings relevant and helpful in our daily lives.

With thought-provoking statements and revelatory explanations, quotations from the Bible and the Bhagavad Gita, and incidents from the lives of great souls, Paramahamsa Prajnanananda distils the wisdom of the ages into clear, relevant instructions on leading a moral and spiritual life in the world today. Without being overly pedantic, yet incorporating the texts of countless scriptures within his lectures, Paramahamsa Prajnanandaji does what most religious teachers stop short of doing and what most of us are thirsting for: he gives step by step methods for achieving self-realization. Gearing his lectures to the modern world of East and West, peppering them with colourful anecdotes, in his humorous yet compassionate style, with constant words of encouragement to those who must continue to live in the world, he guides disciples with the love of a mother. To those who are baffled by the vastness of ancient scriptural wisdom, the clear, concise and immensely helpful hints and guidance he provides, helps to make sense of book learning.

The power of his teachings lies in their simplicity and direct relevance to our lives. He teaches one of the simplest truths of the scriptures. One needs not only the desire for salvation, but also the guidance of the Guru and the regular practice of meditation and then and only then comes realization.

Paramahamsa Prajnanananda teaches only one lesson: the lesson of love. Through not only the study of scriptures, and the practice of meditation, but through every action and every breath, he urges us to realize that we are all divine and to achieve that blissful state of divine love and contentment, through basic self-discipline and the practice of simple *yogic* principles.

His loving guidance and deep compassion have won him the devotion and faith of countless disciples around the world whose lives he has transformed.

KRIYA YOGA

The ancient history of Kriya Yoga is mystifying and mesmerizing. Its mysterious origins are an intermingling of mythology, history, and science that date from the dawn of human consciousness. Saints and sages of India have long practiced and spread the science of yoga. Kriya Yoga is a very ancient and effective yogic science as well as an age-old tradition that has been practiced by seers, saints, and sages since time immemorial.

In Indian mythology, even Rama and Krishna practiced and taught the Kriya meditation technique. Kriya practices were explained by the rishis in the Upanishads, by Sage Vasishtha in Yoga Vasishtha, and by Maharshi Patañjali in his Yoga Sutra.

The Bhagavad Gita (4:1) says that God first revealed the Kriya technique to Vivashvan, then Vivashvan passed it to his son Manu, the seventh of the fourteen Manus or progenitors of the human race. Manu then transmitted it to his son Ikshvaku, founder of the first dynasty of kings in ancient India. From then on this technique was transmitted from father to son, which metaphorically means from master to disciple, through direct oral transmission. Apparently lost in the increasing spiritual decline of later epochs, these teachings were revived by the timeless Mahavatar Babaji Maharaj in 1861, who named the technique "Kriya Yoga."

KRIYA YOGA CONTACTS

Kriya Yoga Centre Vienna
Pottendorferstrasse 69 A-2523 Tattendorf Austria
Tel: 0043 2253 81491   Fax: 0043 2253 80462
E-mail: kriya.yoga.centre@aon.at   Web:www.kriyayoga-europe.org

Hariharananda Gurukulam
P.O. Chaitana, Balighai, Puri 750002, Orissa, India
Tel/Fax: 0091 6752 246644   Tel/Fax: 0091 6752 246788
E-mail: pmission@sify.com   Web: www.prajnanamission.org

KRIYA YOGA CONTACTS

Kriya Yoga Institute
P.O. Box 924615 Homestead, FL 33092-4615 USA
Tel: 001 305 2471960 Fax: 001 305 2481951
E-mail: institute@kriya.org   Web: www.kriya.org

Kriya Yoga Center
Heezerweg 7, Sterksel, NL-6029 PP, Holland
Tel: 0031 40 2265576 Fax: 0031 40 2265612
E-mail: kriya.yoga@worldonline.nl

OTHER BOOKS BY PARAMAHAMSA PRAJNANANANDA

Mahavatar Babaji: The Eternal Light of God, ISBN 81-86713-06-9
Lahiri Mahasaya: Fountainhead of Kriya Yoga, ISBN 3-901665-22-6
Swami Shriyukteshwar: Incarnation of Wisdom, ISBN 3-901665-23-4
Paramahamsa Hariharananda: River of Compassion, ISBN 3-901665-24-2
The Lineage of Kriya Yoga Masters, ISBN 3-902038-13-6
My Time with the Master, ISBN 3-902038-08-X
Discourses on the Bhagavad Gita, Volume I, ISBN 3-901665-25-0, Volume II, ISBN 3-901665-26-9
The Torah, The Bible and Kriya Yoga, ISBN 81-86713-00-X
Rama Katha, ISBN 3-902038-23-3
Yoga Pathway of the Divine ISBN 3-901665-21-8
The Path of Love, ISBN 3-902038-07-1
Life and Values, ISBN 3-902038-09-8
Akshara Tattva, ISBN 81-87825-02-2
Nava Durga: The Multiple Forms of the Mother, ISBN 3-901665-28-5
Nectar Drops: Sayings of Paramahamsa Hariharananda, ISBN 3-901665-01-3
Words of Wisdom: Stories and Parables of Paramahamsa Hariharananda, ISBN 3-901665-00-5
Krishna Katha, ISBN 1-931733-00-7
A Successful Lifestyle, ISBN 3-902038-26-8
Daily Prayers, ISBN 1-931733-02-3
The Changing Nature of Relationships, ISBN 3-902038-10-1
Prapanna Gita, ISBN 1-971733-01-5
Daily Reflections, ISBN 3-902038-12-8
Kriya Yoga: Path of Soul Culture, ISBN 81-87825-07-3
Gautama Buddha, ISBN 3-902038-16-0
The Body's Dance, the Soul's Play, ISBN 3-902038-17-9
Jnana Sankalini Tantra, PB ISBN 3-902038-18-7, HB 3-902038-20-9
The Last Decade, A Loving Recollection ISBN 3-902038-24-1